MOVING TO C

A COMPREHENSIVE GUIDE

BY

WILLIAM JONES

2024

Moving to Cyprus: A Comprehensive Guide by William Jones
This book edition was created and published by Mamba Press
©MambaPress 2024. All Rights Reserved.

Contents

Preface

Moving to a new country is like stepping into an unwritten chapter of your life, an adventure waiting to unfold. As you hold this guide in your hands, contemplating a move to the captivating island of Cyprus, I want to assure you that you're about to embark on a journey filled with excitement, challenges, and a profound sense of discovery. In these pages, we'll explore the nuances of life in Cyprus, the practicalities of relocation, and the intangible aspects that transform a foreign place into a new home.

The decision to move is never an easy one. It involves leaving behind the familiar, stepping into the unknown, and embracing change. But it's precisely in these moments of uncertainty that life's most enriching experiences are often found. Cyprus, with its history stretching back millennia, its warm Mediterranean embrace, and its diverse cultural tapestry, offers a unique canvas for your next chapter.

I'm not here to offer you a one-size-fits-all manual but rather a companion on your journey. Consider me your virtual friend, a fellow traveler who has walked the winding streets of unfamiliar cities, navigated bureaucratic mazes, and marveled at the breathtaking landscapes this world has to offer. In these 3000 words, I hope to share not just practical advice but the essence of what it means to immerse yourself in a new culture, to learn, to adapt, and ultimately, to thrive.

Cyprus, with its sun-kissed shores and storied past, beckons you. Before we delve into the nitty-gritty details, let's take a moment to appreciate the tapestry of experiences awaiting you.

Imagine waking up to the gentle sound of waves lapping against the shore, a sun that seems to have reserved its brightest rays just for you. Picture yourself strolling through ancient streets, where the whispers of history echo in the stones beneath your feet. Envision savoring the flavors of Mediterranean cuisine, each dish a delicious blend of tradition and innovation. Cyprus isn't just a destination; it's an invitation to create a life infused with culture, warmth, and moments that linger in your memory.

This guide is more than a roadmap; it's a collection of stories, insights, and practical wisdom gathered from those who have ventured before you. From the complexities of paperwork to the joy of discovering hidden gems in your new neighborhood, every chapter is crafted with the intention of easing your transition.

As you flip through these pages, you'll find advice on everything from finding a place to call home and navigating the job market to embracing the local culture and making lasting connections. But beyond the logistical details, I want to share the intangible aspects of relocation – the moments of uncertainty, the triumphs of overcoming challenges, and the joy of building a life that reflects your unique journey.

Moving to a new country is more than a change of address; it's a profound transformation. It's about finding your place in a world that is both different and wonderfully the same. It's about forging connections, broadening your horizons, and discovering the strength within yourself to navigate the uncharted.

In these pages, you'll find not just information but a celebration of the human spirit's capacity to adapt and thrive. You're not alone in this adventure. Many have walked this path before you, each with their own story, and now it's your turn to inscribe your narrative into the vibrant tapestry of expatriate life.

As we embark on this journey together, remember that the key to a successful move lies not just in the practicalities but in embracing the spirit of exploration. Cyprus awaits, ready to unveil its wonders and welcome you into its embrace. So, let's turn the page, step into the unknown, and savor the unfolding chapters of your life on this enchanting Mediterranean island. Welcome to your Cyprus adventure.

Introduction

Welcome, fellow adventurer, to the beginning of a transformative journey. As you stand on the precipice of relocating to Cyprus, the air is thick with anticipation, and I can almost sense the mixture of excitement and trepidation pulsating through you. Let me assure you, this journey you're about to embark upon is more than a change of scenery; it's an odyssey, an exploration of the self in the midst of a new world.

In these next few thousand words, we're going to unravel the mysteries of Cyprus together. This sun-soaked island, nestled in the azure embrace of the Mediterranean, is not just a destination; it's an invitation to rediscover life in all its richness. As we navigate the intricacies of your impending move, I want you to keep one thing in mind – this isn't just about logistics and paperwork; it's about crafting a story, a narrative uniquely yours, set against the backdrop of this captivating land.

Picture Cyprus in your mind. Envision the sunlight playing on the cerulean sea, casting a shimmering dance of diamonds on the water. Think of ancient ruins that tell tales of civilizations long gone, standing as silent witnesses to the passage of time. Imagine the aroma of olive groves and the taste of halloumi, each bite a celebration of the island's rich culinary heritage. This is the canvas upon which you are about to paint the next chapter of your life.

So, why Cyprus? What magic does this island hold that beckons travelers from every corner of the globe? Let me paint a picture for you.

A Tapestry of History and Culture

Cyprus isn't just an island; it's a living testament to the ebb and flow of civilizations. As you explore its historical sites, from the ancient city of Kourion to the medieval charm of Kyrenia, you'll find yourself stepping into the footprints of Phoenicians, Romans, Byzantines, and more. It's a place where history is not confined to textbooks but is etched into the very stones beneath your feet.

The cultural mosaic of Cyprus is equally enchanting. The warmth of Cypriot hospitality is legendary, and you'll soon find yourself welcomed not just into homes but into a tight-knit community that values connection and camaraderie. From traditional festivals that echo with the joyous beats of music to the simple pleasure of sharing a cup of coffee with newfound friends, Cyprus invites you to immerse yourself in a culture that embraces both tradition and modernity.

Nature's Embrace

Close your eyes and feel the gentle breeze carrying the scent of blooming flowers. Cyprus is a haven for nature lovers, a sanctuary where mountains meet the sea, and landscapes shift from lush greenery to rugged cliffs. The Troodos Mountains, with their pine-covered slopes, provide a stark contrast to the pristine beaches that line the coast. Whether you're an avid hiker or someone who simply enjoys a leisurely stroll, Cyprus offers a canvas of natural beauty that captivates the soul.

And then, there's the sea – a canvas of endless blue. The crystal-clear waters that lap against the shore beckon you to dip your toes into an experience that goes beyond the physical; it's a connection to the very essence of life. Snorkel in hidden coves, sail into the sunset, or simply bask in the warmth of the Mediterranean sun – Cyprus is a sanctuary for those who find solace in nature's embrace.

Culinary Delights

Let's talk about food, a universal language that transcends borders. Cypriot cuisine is a symphony of flavors, a testament to the island's rich agricultural heritage and the influence of various civilizations that have left their mark. From the tangy olives that grace your meze platter to the savory souvlaki sizzling on the grill, each bite is a journey through time and taste.

Halloumi, the squeaky cheese that has become synonymous with Cypriot gastronomy, is just the tip of the culinary iceberg. As you explore local markets and tavernas, you'll discover a wealth of dishes that celebrate the bounty of the land and sea. And let's not forget the sweet indulgence of loukoumades, honey-drenched dough balls that will undoubtedly find a special place in your heart – and your taste buds.

A Mosaic of Experiences

Cyprus is not a static destination; it's a dynamic mosaic of experiences waiting to be discovered. Whether you're a history enthusiast, a nature lover, a culinary connoisseur, or someone simply seeking the warmth of human connection, Cyprus has something to offer.

Now, let's shift our focus to you. Why are you here, contemplating a move to this island paradise? Perhaps it's a career opportunity, a desire for a change of pace, or a quest for personal growth. Whatever the reason, you're on the verge of a profound shift, and I'm here to guide you through the intricacies of this transition.

This guide is not a rulebook; it's a conversation. Together, we'll explore the practical aspects of your move – from understanding the paperwork to finding a place to call home, from navigating the job market to embracing the local culture. But beyond the logistical details, we'll delve into the essence of relocation – the emotions, the challenges, and the triumphs that shape this journey.

As we journey through these pages, remember that this isn't just about moving to a new country; it's about becoming a part of a living, breathing community. It's about discovering not just the external landscapes of Cyprus but the internal landscapes of yourself. So, as we step into the labyrinth of relocation, let curiosity be your compass and resilience your guide.

The adventure begins now. Open your heart to the possibilities, for Cyprus awaits with open arms, ready to weave your story into its rich tapestry. Welcome to the unfolding chapters of your life in Cyprus – a journey that promises discovery, growth, and the creation of memories that will last a lifetime.

Chapter 1
Understanding Cyprus

Welcome to the heart of the Mediterranean, where ancient history meets modern allure, and the sun-kissed landscapes unfold stories that echo through the ages. Cyprus, the third-largest island in the Mediterranean Sea, isn't just a destination; it's a living testament to the crossroads of civilizations, a place where myths and legends intertwine with the vibrant tapestry of contemporary life.

A Tapestry of History

Let's embark on a journey through time, where the threads of history weave together to create the rich fabric that is Cyprus. The island's story is as diverse and layered as the landscapes that stretch from its coastline to the mountainous interior.

Imagine standing on the sunlit grounds of Kourion, an ancient city that dates back to the Hellenistic period. As you wander through the remnants of grand villas, theaters, and temples, it's as if the stones themselves whisper tales of a bygone era. The Romans, who once walked these streets, left their mark in the form of intricate mosaics that paint vivid portraits of daily life.

Fast forward to the medieval charm of Kyrenia, where a picturesque harbor welcomes you with open arms. The Kyrenia Castle, standing proudly against the backdrop of the sea, tells tales of Byzantine, Lusignan, and Ottoman rule. Each conqueror brought a piece of their culture, leaving an indelible imprint on the island's identity.

And then there's Nicosia, the divided capital, where the Green Line serves as a poignant reminder of the complex political history that Cyprus has navigated in recent decades. Stroll through the narrow streets of the Old Town, where ancient city walls coexist with modern cafes, creating a seamless blend of the past and the present.

The Crossroads of Civilizations

Cyprus, with its strategic location, has been a coveted prize for empires and nations throughout history. Phoenicians, Assyrians, Egyptians, Persians, and Alexander the Great – each left their mark on this island, contributing to its cultural mosaic. The Byzantines, who followed, adorned the land with intricate frescoes and Byzantine-style churches, some of which are now UNESCO World Heritage sites.

Venture into the medieval period, and you'll encounter the Crusaders, whose castles dot the landscape, standing as silent sentinels of a tumultuous era. As the Ottoman Empire expanded its reach, Cyprus became a part of its territories, adding yet another layer to its cultural identity.

In 1878, the island came under British administration, a period that left its mark on governance, education, and even the sport of cricket – an unexpected but enduring legacy. The struggle for independence in the mid-20th century shaped Cyprus into the nation we know today, a Republic in the sun-drenched embrace of the Mediterranean.

Geography and Regions

As you prepare to make Cyprus your home, understanding its geography is key to navigating its diverse landscapes. The island is divided into six administrative regions, each with its own unique charm.

1. Nicosia (Lefkosia): The capital city, situated in the center of the island, is a bustling metropolis with a rich historical core. Divided between the Republic of Cyprus and the Turkish Republic of Northern Cyprus, Nicosia is a city of contrasts, where modernity coexists with ancient traditions.

2. Limassol (Lemesos): Head south, and you'll find Limassol, a vibrant coastal city known for its lively atmosphere and long stretches of sandy beaches. The Limassol Marina offers a taste of luxury, while the Old Town invites you to wander through narrow streets lined with charming boutiques and cafes.

3. Larnaca (Larnaka): With its international airport, Larnaca is often the first point of entry for many travelers. Beyond being a transportation hub, Larnaca boasts a beautiful promenade, historic sites like the Church of Saint Lazarus, and the allure of the Hala Sultan Tekke mosque on the salt lake.

4. Paphos: A UNESCO World Heritage site, Paphos is a treasure trove of archaeological wonders, from the Tombs of the Kings to the intricate mosaics of the House of Dionysus. This region, on the western coast, is a haven for history enthusiasts and beach lovers alike.

5. Famagusta (Gazimağusa): To the east lies Famagusta, a city with a rich history and a coastline that beckons with golden beaches. The city walls and the medieval Othello Castle speak of an era long past, while the nearby Salamis ruins provide a glimpse into ancient civilizations.

6. Kyrenia (Girne): In the northern part of the island, Kyrenia stands as a beacon of maritime charm. The harbor, with its iconic castle, sets the stage for a picturesque backdrop. Kyrenia is a gateway to the stunning landscapes of the Kyrenia Range and the untouched beauty of the Karpas Peninsula.

A Feast for the Senses: Cuisine and Culture

Now, let's shift our focus from the echoes of the past to the vibrant pulse of contemporary life in Cyprus. One of the most delightful aspects of immersing yourself in a new culture is savoring its culinary treasures, and Cyprus is a feast for the senses.

Meze Magic: When it comes to dining in Cyprus, be prepared for a culinary journey that goes beyond the plate. Meze, a traditional style of dining, invites you to sample a variety of small dishes, each bursting with flavor. From creamy hummus and smoky baba ganoush to succulent kebabs and grilled halloumi, meze is a celebration of diversity, a reflection of the island's multicultural history.

Halloumi Heaven: Speaking of halloumi, prepare to fall in love with this iconic Cypriot cheese. The squeaky delight of fresh halloumi, grilled to perfection, is a culinary experience that lingers on your taste buds. Whether enjoyed on its own or as part of a meze platter, halloumi is a symbol of Cyprus's culinary prowess.

Cyprus Delights: No culinary exploration is complete without indulging in Cyprus's sweet delights. Loukoumades, golden balls of dough drizzled with honey, and baklava, layered with nuts and syrup, are treats that will transport your taste buds to a sugary haven. Pair these delights with a strong cup of Cypriot coffee, and you have the perfect ending to a delightful meal.

Local Libations: Wash down your culinary adventures with local libations that showcase the island's diverse influences. Commandaria, a sweet wine with a history dating back to the Knights Templar, is one of the oldest wines still in production. And of course, no gathering is complete without a toast of zivania, a potent grape-based spirit that embodies the spirit of celebration.

Cypriot Hospitality: A Warm Embrace

Beyond the historical sites and culinary wonders, what truly defines Cyprus is the warmth of its people. Cypriots are renowned for their hospitality, a trait deeply ingrained in the fabric of their culture. As you navigate the streets of Nicosia or share a meal in a village taverna, you'll find yourself welcomed not as a stranger but as a friend.

Hospitality in Cyprus goes beyond mere politeness; it's an invitation to connect, to share stories, and to forge meaningful relationships. Don't be surprised if a casual conversation with a local turns into an invitation to a family gathering or a guided tour of hidden gems.

The Language of Cyprus: A Blend of Cultures

While Greek is the official language of Cyprus, you'll find a linguistic tapestry woven with influences from various cultures. English is widely spoken, particularly in urban areas and tourist hotspots. Additionally, you might encounter traces of Turkish, reflecting the island's complex history.

Learning a few basic Greek phrases will undoubtedly enhance your experience and open doors to deeper connections. Cypriots appreciate the effort, and a simple "Kalimera" (good morning) or "Efharisto" (thank you) can go a long way in bridging cultural gaps.

Navigating Daily Life

As you prepare for your adventure in Cyprus, it's essential to understand the practicalities of daily life. From transportation to healthcare, familiarizing yourself with the essentials will pave the way for a smoother transition.

Transportation: Cyprus offers a well-developed transportation infrastructure, making it relatively easy to navigate the island. Public buses connect major cities and towns, providing an affordable and convenient mode of transportation. Renting a car is a popular choice for exploring more remote areas, especially if you plan to delve into the mountainous regions or uncover secluded beaches.

Driving in Cyprus follows the left-hand side of the road, and road signs are in both Greek and English. The island's relatively compact size means that you can traverse from coast to mountain in a matter of hours, allowing you to explore its diverse landscapes at your own pace.

Healthcare: Cyprus boasts a modern healthcare system, with public and private options available. The public healthcare system is accessible to residents who contribute to the social insurance fund. Expatriates often opt for private healthcare, which provides a range of services and faster access to medical facilities.

Pharmacies are abundant, and many medications that require a prescription in other countries can be obtained over the counter in Cyprus. It's advisable to have comprehensive health insurance to cover any unexpected medical expenses.

Cost of Living: The cost of living in Cyprus varies depending on factors such as location, lifestyle, and housing choices. While certain aspects, such as groceries and dining out, may be comparable to other European countries, goods that need to be imported can be more expensive.

Renting a home is a significant consideration, and prices fluctuate based on location and property size. Researching local markets and understanding the cost of living in your chosen region will help you budget effectively.

Cultural Etiquette: Cyprus, with its blend of cultures, has its own set of social customs and etiquette. Greetings are warm and often accompanied by a handshake or a kiss on both cheeks, particularly in more casual settings. It's customary to remove your shoes when entering someone's home.

Tipping is generally expected, with 10% to 15% considered standard in restaurants. When invited to a Cypriot home, it's polite to bring a small gift as a token of appreciation.

Embracing the Mediterranean Lifestyle

As you delve into the intricacies of life in Cyprus, remember that it's not just about adapting to a new set of circumstances; it's about embracing a lifestyle shaped by the Mediterranean rhythm. The concept of "siga-siga," meaning slowly-slowly, is a reminder to savor the moment, to appreciate the beauty in simplicity.

Take the time to explore local markets, where vendors proudly display their fresh produce and handmade crafts. Attend traditional festivals, where the air is filled with the sounds of music and the aroma of local delicacies. Join in the joyous celebrations of Easter, marked by religious processions and feasts that bring communities together.

Chapter in Review

In this exploration of Cyprus, we've traversed through time, unraveling the historical tapestry that adorns the island. We've savored the flavors of Cypriot cuisine, indulged in the warmth of Cypriot hospitality, and navigated the practicalities of daily life. Cyprus isn't just a destination; it's an immersive experience, an invitation to write your story against the backdrop of its rich landscapes and vibrant culture.

As you prepare to make Cyprus your home, remember that understanding goes hand in hand with appreciation. The more you delve into the layers of this island, the more it reveals its magic. Whether you find yourself captivated by the ancient ruins of Salamis, enchanted by the aroma of souvlaki on a seaside grill, or embraced by the warmth of Cypriot smiles, you're on the threshold of a chapter that promises discovery, growth, and the creation of memories that will last a lifetime.

So, dear traveler, as you stand at the crossroads of past and present, let the spirit of Cyprus beckon you. Open your heart to the possibilities, for this island is more than a destination; it's a canvas waiting for the brushstrokes of your experiences to create a masterpiece of a life well-lived. Welcome to the embrace of Cyprus – a journey that begins with understanding and unfolds with every step you take in this captivating land.

Chapter 2

Planning Your Move

Congratulations! You've made the exciting decision to embark on a new chapter of your life, and Cyprus is beckoning with its sun-soaked shores and rich cultural tapestry. As you stand on the threshold of this adventure, planning becomes the compass that guides your journey. In this chapter, we'll dive into the intricacies of preparing for your move to Cyprus – from the initial research phase to navigating the bureaucratic nuances. So, let's roll up our sleeves and get ready to turn your dream of living in Cyprus into a well-thought-out reality.

Researching Your New Home

The first step in any successful move is understanding the lay of the land. Cyprus, with its diverse regions and cities, offers a myriad of options to suit different preferences. Whether you're drawn to the bustling streets of Nicosia, the coastal charm of Limassol, or the historical allure of Paphos, each region has its unique character.

Start your research by delving into the specifics of each area. Consider factors such as climate, amenities, and lifestyle. Are you someone who thrives in a vibrant urban setting, or do you yearn for the tranquility of a seaside village? Cyprus has a place for every taste, and this decision sets the tone for your entire experience.

Think about your daily commute, access to healthcare, and proximity to schools if you have children. Take a virtual stroll through neighborhoods using online maps and explore local forums to gain insights from current residents. This initial research phase lays the foundation for a smooth transition, helping you choose a location that aligns with your preferences and needs.

Understanding Legal Requirements

Ah, the bureaucracy – a necessary dance in the process of moving to a new country. Cyprus, like any other destination, has its set of legal requirements, and understanding these from the outset can save you from last-minute surprises.

For most travelers, the entry point is securing the appropriate visa. The type of visa you'll need depends on your reason for moving – whether it's for employment, retirement, or studying. Cyprus offers various visa options, including the Long-Term Residence Permit and the Cyprus Investment Program for those looking to make a significant investment in the country.

For European Union (EU) citizens, the process is relatively straightforward, thanks to the free movement agreements within the EU. Non-EU citizens may need to navigate a more intricate process, so it's advisable to consult with the nearest Cypriot embassy or consulate well in advance.

Once you've sorted out the visa requirements, turn your attention to the practical aspects. Consider opening a Cypriot bank account, which will be essential for managing your finances and handling local transactions. Familiarize yourself with the tax regulations in Cyprus, including any obligations you may have in your home country.

Navigating the Housing Market

Now, let's talk about your new home. The housing market in Cyprus is diverse, offering options ranging from apartments in urban centers to villas in more secluded areas. The key to finding the perfect abode is to start your search early and explore different neighborhoods.

Online platforms, local real estate agents, and expat forums are valuable resources in your quest for the ideal home. Take virtual tours, connect with local real estate professionals, and gather as much information as possible. Keep in mind factors like proximity to amenities, public transportation, and the overall atmosphere of the neighborhood.

Renting or buying – the choice depends on your long-term plans and financial considerations. Renting is often the preferred initial step, allowing you to acclimate to your chosen area before making a more significant commitment. If you decide to buy, enlist the services of a reputable local real estate agent who can guide you through the process and help you navigate any potential language barriers.

Job Market and Networking

If your move is tied to employment, understanding the job market in Cyprus is crucial. Research industries that are thriving, explore job opportunities, and update your resume accordingly. Online job portals and industry-specific forums are excellent tools for connecting with potential employers and understanding the current job landscape.

Networking is a golden key in any job search, and Cyprus is no exception. Attend industry events, join professional organizations, and leverage social media platforms to connect with professionals in your field. Personal connections often play a significant role in the Cypriot job market, so don't underestimate the power of a friendly conversation or a well-crafted LinkedIn profile.

Schools and Education

If you have children or are planning to pursue education yourself, understanding the education system in Cyprus is paramount. The island offers a mix of public and private schools, each with its unique curriculum and ethos.

Research schools in your chosen area, considering factors such as academic reputation, extracurricular activities, and language of instruction. Schedule visits or virtual meetings with school administrators to get a feel for the educational environment and ensure that it aligns with your family's values and goals.

For those pursuing higher education, Cyprus has universities and institutions that cater to a diverse range of disciplines. Explore academic programs, admission requirements, and scholarship opportunities to plan your educational journey effectively.

Healthcare and Insurance

Access to quality healthcare is a fundamental aspect of any relocation. Cyprus boasts a modern healthcare system with both public and private options. Expatriates often opt for private healthcare, which provides quicker access to medical services and a broader range of facilities.

Enroll in the Cypriot public healthcare system if you're eligible, or explore private health insurance options to ensure comprehensive coverage. Familiarize yourself with the locations of nearby hospitals and clinics, and keep emergency contact numbers readily available.

Financial Considerations

Managing your finances effectively is a cornerstone of a successful move. Cyprus, like any other country, has its nuances when it comes to banking, taxes, and daily expenses.

Open a local bank account as soon as possible, as this will streamline financial transactions and ease the process of receiving your salary, if applicable. Explore different banks to find one that aligns with your needs and offers the services you require.

Understand the tax regulations in Cyprus and any obligations you may have in your home country. Seeking the advice of a tax professional can provide clarity and help you optimize your financial situation.

Create a budget that encompasses all aspects of daily life, from housing and utilities to transportation and entertainment. This will give you a clear picture of your financial landscape and help you adjust your spending habits accordingly.

Language and Communication

While English is widely spoken in Cyprus, particularly in urban areas, making an effort to learn a few basic Greek phrases can enhance your experience and foster connections with the local community. The official languages are Greek and Turkish, reflecting the island's complex history.

Consider enrolling in language classes or using language learning apps to familiarize yourself with everyday expressions. Cypriots appreciate the effort, and even a simple greeting in Greek can go a long way in building rapport.

Cultural Integration and Socializing

Beyond the practicalities, cultural integration is the heartbeat of a fulfilling expatriate experience. Cyprus, with its warm and welcoming culture, invites you to become a part of its vibrant community.

Attend local events, festivals, and gatherings to immerse yourself in the Cypriot way of life. Participate in community activities, join clubs or groups aligned with your interests, and be open to making new friends. The more you engage with the local community, the richer your experience will be.

Transportation: Navigating the Roads

Understanding transportation options is essential for seamless daily living in Cyprus. While public buses connect major cities and towns, many residents opt for private transportation, especially in more rural areas.

If you plan to drive, familiarize yourself with the rules of the road and the local driving culture. Cyprus follows the left-hand driving system, and road signs are in both Greek and English. Renting a car is a popular choice for exploring the island's hidden gems, from mountain villages to secluded beaches.

Leisure and Recreation

Life in Cyprus isn't just about work and practicalities; it's about savoring the beauty of the island and enjoying leisure time. Whether you're an outdoor enthusiast, a history buff, or someone who simply appreciates a good meal, Cyprus offers a plethora of activities to suit every taste.

Explore hiking trails in the Troodos Mountains, relax on the pristine beaches of Ayia Napa, or indulge in a leisurely stroll through the historic streets of Larnaca. Attend cultural events, visit archaeological sites, and savor the diverse culinary delights that Cyprus has to offer.

Dealing with Challenges

No move is without its challenges, and understanding that bumps along the road are part of the journey will help you navigate them with resilience. Whether it's adapting to a new work culture, overcoming language barriers, or facing homesickness, it's essential to approach challenges with a positive mindset.

Build a support system of fellow expatriates, connect with locals who have faced similar challenges, and seek guidance from professionals or support services if needed. Remember that challenges are opportunities for growth, and each hurdle you overcome adds depth to your expatriate experience.

Chapter in Review

As we wrap up our journey through the planning phase, take a moment to reflect on the groundwork you've laid. From researching your new home to understanding legal requirements, finding accommodation, and preparing for the cultural transition – each step is a brushstroke on the canvas of your Cypriot adventure.

Planning your move is not just about logistics; it's about setting the stage for a life filled with exploration, connection, and meaningful experiences. As you navigate the intricacies of relocation, keep in mind that every challenge is an opportunity, and every decision is a step toward the life you envision in Cyprus.

The road ahead is paved with the promise of discovery and growth. The practicalities are stepping stones, and the real magic lies in the moments of connection, the shared laughter, and the unfolding chapters of your Cypriot story. So, with your plans in place and a sense of anticipation in your heart, step boldly into the next chapter – the chapter where Cyprus becomes not just a destination but a cherished part of your life's journey. Welcome to the adventure!

Chapter 3
Finding Accommodation

Ah, the quest for the perfect abode – it's a journey that carries both the thrill of anticipation and the weight of practical considerations. As you embark on this chapter of your Cypriot adventure, finding the right accommodation becomes a pivotal piece of the puzzle. It's not just about a place to rest your head; it's about creating a home that resonates with your lifestyle and aligns with the rhythm of your new surroundings.

Understanding the Landscape

Before we dive into the nitty-gritty of property hunting, let's take a moment to understand the diverse landscape of accommodation options in Cyprus. From bustling urban centers to quaint coastal villages and serene mountain retreats, the island offers a spectrum of choices to suit every taste.

In cities like Nicosia, Limassol, and Larnaca, you'll find a mix of apartments, townhouses, and modern developments. These urban hubs are characterized by their vibrant energy, proximity to amenities, and a cosmopolitan atmosphere. If you're drawn to the lull of the waves and the salty breeze, coastal towns like Paphos, Limassol, and Larnaca beckon with seaside apartments and villas. For those seeking tranquility in the embrace of nature, the mountainous regions, particularly around Troodos, offer picturesque villages and rustic homes.

Consider your lifestyle preferences, commute requirements, and the atmosphere you envision for your daily life. Each region in Cyprus tells a different story, and choosing the right setting sets the stage for a fulfilling chapter in your expatriate journey.

Renting vs. Buying: Deciding Your Path

The age-old debate – to rent or to buy? This decision often hinges on your long-term plans, financial considerations, and the level of commitment you're comfortable with.

Renting is a popular choice for many newcomers, offering flexibility and the opportunity to explore different neighborhoods before making a more significant commitment. Apartments, townhouses, and even standalone villas are available for rent, and the lease terms can vary from short-term to long-term agreements.

Buying a property is a more substantial investment, and it's a route often taken by those who see Cyprus as their long-term home. The island's real estate market is diverse, with options ranging from modern developments to traditional homes with a historical charm. Engaging with a reputable local real estate agent becomes invaluable in navigating the complexities of property ownership.

Consider your budget, weigh the pros and cons of each option, and envision the lifestyle you desire. Whether you're testing the waters with a rental or diving into the commitment of ownership, Cyprus offers a housing market that caters to a spectrum of needs.

Navigating Online Platforms and Real Estate Agents

Welcome to the digital age, where property hunting has become a virtual adventure. Online platforms and real estate websites are treasure troves of information, allowing you to explore properties from the comfort of your current abode. From panoramic images to detailed descriptions, these platforms provide a sneak peek into the available options.

Popular real estate websites in Cyprus include platforms like Property Cyprus, Bazaraki, and Rightmove Cyprus. These platforms categorize properties based on location, type, and price range, offering a user-friendly interface to filter through the myriad of options.

While virtual exploration is an excellent starting point, engaging with a local real estate agent adds a layer of expertise and insight. These professionals have an intimate knowledge of the local market, can guide you through the nuances of property transactions, and often have access to listings that may not be publicly available.

Real estate agents become your partners in the journey, helping you navigate language barriers, negotiating on your behalf, and providing valuable advice on the intricacies of the Cypriot property landscape. Establishing a connection with a trusted agent can turn the property search into a collaborative and personalized experience.

Considering Budget and Hidden Costs

Ah, the ever-present budget – the compass that guides your property hunt. Before you dive into the world of viewings and negotiations, it's crucial to establish a realistic budget that encompasses all aspects of accommodation.

Consider not only the monthly rent or property purchase price but also additional costs that may sneak up on you. For renters, this could include utility bills, common expenses in apartment buildings, and any potential maintenance fees. For buyers, there are property transfer fees, stamp duty, and legal fees that need to be factored into the equation.

As you set your budget, be mindful of the overall cost of living in your chosen area. Different regions in Cyprus may have varying price ranges, and understanding the local economy will help you make an informed decision.

Viewings: The Exciting Exploration

With your budget in hand and online research under your belt, it's time for the exciting phase – property viewings. This is your chance to step into the physical space, feel the ambiance, and envision yourself calling this place home.

When attending viewings, come prepared with a list of questions and considerations. Pay attention to the condition of the property, the neighborhood atmosphere, and the accessibility of amenities. Take note of any potential maintenance issues or renovations that may be needed.

Feel free to engage with the current occupants or neighbors if possible. They can provide valuable insights into the community dynamics, the quirks of the property, and any aspects that may not be apparent during a brief viewing.

Remember that finding the perfect accommodation is a blend of practical considerations and a gut feeling. Trust your instincts, ask the necessary questions, and allow yourself to visualize the space as your own.

Negotiating the Deal

Once you've identified a property that aligns with your vision, it's time to enter the negotiation phase. Whether you're renting or buying, negotiating is a delicate dance that requires finesse and a clear understanding of your priorities.

For renters, negotiate the monthly rent, lease terms, and any additional costs. Landlords may be open to discussing terms, especially if you're signing a longer lease or can offer assurances of financial stability.

For buyers, negotiations often extend beyond the purchase price. Property transfer fees, the timing of the transaction, and potential renovations may all be on the table. Engage with your real estate agent to navigate these negotiations effectively and ensure that the final agreement aligns with your expectations.

Legalities and Contracts

As you move closer to sealing the deal, legalities come into play. For renters, this involves reviewing and signing a lease agreement that outlines the terms and conditions of your tenancy. Ensure that you understand the clauses, particularly those related to maintenance responsibilities, lease duration, and any penalties for early termination.

Buyers, on the other hand, will engage in a more intricate legal process. The property purchase agreement, known as the Sales Agreement, outlines the terms of the sale, including the purchase price, payment schedule, and any conditions that need to be met. Legal professionals play a crucial role in this phase, conducting due diligence, ensuring that the property has a clear title, and guiding you through the intricacies of the transaction.

Engage with a reputable lawyer who specializes in real estate trans-actions to ensure a smooth and legally sound process. Their expertise becomes your safeguard, offering peace of mind as you transition from negotiations to the finalization of the deal.

Moving In: The Transition to Your New Home

With the deal sealed and legalities squared away, the moment ar-rives – it's time to move into your new home. Whether you're unpack-ing suitcases or overseeing a team of movers, the transition to your Cypriot abode is a significant milestone.

Take the time to settle in, explore your neighborhood, and gradual-ly weave your routine into the fabric of your new surroundings. Famil-iarize yourself with local markets, discover hidden gems, and embrace the sense of community that Cyprus has to offer.

Consider reaching out to neighbors, attending local events, and immersing yourself in the cultural tapestry of your new home. This isn't just a place to reside; it's a canvas waiting for the brushstrokes of your experiences to create a masterpiece of a life well-lived.

Dealing with Challenges and Celebrating Milestones

As with any significant transition, challenges may arise, and it's es-sential to approach them with resilience and a problem-solving mind-set. Whether it's adjusting to a new work culture, navigating language barriers, or dealing with homesickness, remember that each challenge is an opportunity for growth.

Celebrate the milestones along the way – the first dinner in your new kitchen, the first sunrise over your balcony, and the moments of connection with neighbors. Embrace the journey, for finding accom-modation in Cyprus isn't just a logistical step; it's an invitation to create a haven that reflects your aspirations and embodies the spirit of your new life.

Chapter in Review

As we conclude our exploration of finding accommodation in Cyprus, take a moment to reflect on the steps you've taken. From understanding the diverse landscape to navigating online platforms, engaging with real estate agents, negotiating deals, and finally settling into your new home – each phase is a chapter in your Cypriot story.

Accommodation isn't just about walls and a roof; it's about the spaces where memories are made, where laughter echoes, and where the chapters of your life unfold. Whether you're renting a cozy apartment in the heart of Nicosia or buying a villa overlooking the Mediterranean in Limassol, Cyprus offers a canvas for you to paint the picture of your dreams.

So, dear traveler, with the keys to your Cypriot abode in hand, step into this new chapter with a sense of excitement and the knowledge that you've laid the foundation for a life enriched by the beauty of Cyprus. Welcome home!

Chapter 4
Navigating the Job Market

Ah, the prospect of a new career adventure on the sun-soaked island of Cyprus! Whether you're seeking new horizons, exploring opportunities in a different field, or simply looking to continue your professional journey, navigating the job market is a crucial step in your expatriate experience. As you step into this chapter, envision it as a canvas waiting for the brushstrokes of your skills, aspirations, and passions. Let's embark on this journey together, exploring the intricacies of the Cypriot job market, creating connections, and embracing the professional landscape that awaits.

Understanding the Professional Landscape

Before we dive into the realm of job hunting, let's take a moment to understand the professional landscape of Cyprus. The island boasts a diverse economy, with key sectors including tourism, shipping, finance, and services. The bustling cities, particularly Nicosia and Limassol, serve as business hubs, hosting a range of industries and companies.

The tourism sector, fueled by the island's natural beauty and rich cultural heritage, is a significant contributor to the economy. From hotels and restaurants to tour operators and event management, opportunities abound for those with a passion for hospitality and tourism.

The maritime industry, anchored by the strategic location of Cyprus, plays a pivotal role. Shipping companies, maritime services, and related industries offer career paths for individuals with expertise in logistics, finance, and international trade.

Finance and services thrive in the urban centers, particularly in Limassol, which is home to a burgeoning financial district. Banking, finance, legal services, and technology companies form a dynamic professional landscape, attracting both local talent and expatriates.

Research the industries that align with your skills and interests, and consider how your expertise can contribute to the vibrant tapestry of Cyprus's professional environment. The more you understand the local job market, the better equipped you'll be to carve out your niche.

Language Skills: A Valuable Asset

As you navigate the job market in Cyprus, language skills become a valuable asset. While English is widely spoken, particularly in business and tourist areas, knowledge of Greek can enhance your opportunities and open doors to a broader range of positions.

Consider investing time in learning basic Greek phrases, as this demonstrates your commitment to assimilating into the local culture. Language proficiency not only enhances your professional standing but also facilitates smoother interactions with colleagues and clients.

Don't let language barriers deter you; view them as an opportunity to enrich your expatriate experience. Engage in language classes, use language learning apps, and immerse yourself in conversations with locals to hone your language skills.

Job Search Strategies

Now, let's embark on the exciting journey of job hunting in Cyprus. The strategies you employ will depend on your field, experience level, and the type of positions you're seeking. Here are some effective approaches to kickstart your job search:

1. **Online Job Portals:** Explore local and international job portals that cater to the Cypriot market. Websites like JobsCyprus, Cyprus Recruiter, and LinkedIn feature job listings across various industries. Create a compelling online profile, upload your resume, and start browsing opportunities that align with your skills.

2. **Networking:** Ah, the power of connections! Networking is a potent tool in the Cypriot job market. Attend industry events, professional gatherings, and networking forums to

build relationships with professionals in your field. Join online groups and forums related to your industry, and don't shy away from reaching out to fellow expatriates who have navigated the job market successfully.

3. **Recruitment Agencies:** Engage with recruitment agencies that specialize in your industry. These professionals have insights into the local job market, maintain relationships with companies, and can connect you with relevant opportunities. Share your career goals, skills, and preferences with the agency, and let them guide you through the job search process.

4. **Company Websites:** Research companies in your industry and explore their official websites. Many organizations post job openings directly on their sites, providing a direct avenue for you to apply. Tailor your resume and cover letter to align with the company's values and requirements, demonstrating your genuine interest in becoming part of their team.

5. **Social Media Presence:** Leverage the power of social media to enhance your job search. Join professional groups on platforms like LinkedIn, engage with industry discussions, and follow companies of interest. Your online presence is an extension of your professional identity, so ensure that your profiles reflect your skills, achievements, and aspirations.

Crafting Your Resume for the Cypriot Market

Your resume is your professional calling card, and tailoring it to the Cypriot market can make a significant difference in attracting the attention of potential employers. Here are some tips for crafting a compelling resume:

1. **Highlight Relevant Experience:** Emphasize experiences that align with the requirements of the Cypriot job market. Showcase your achievements, responsibilities, and the impact

you've had in previous roles.

2. **Include Language Skills:** Clearly indicate your language proficiency, especially if you have a command of Greek. This signals your adaptability and commitment to integrating into the local professional environment.

3. **Quantify Achievements:** Where possible, quantify your achievements. Numbers and statistics provide tangible evidence of your contributions and set you apart from other candidates.

4. **Customize for Each Application:** Tailor your resume for each job application. Align your skills and experiences with the specific requirements of the position, showcasing how you can add value to the company.

5. **Professional Summary:** Craft a concise and impactful professional summary at the beginning of your resume. This section serves as a snapshot of your professional journey and sets the tone for the rest of the document.

Remember that cultural nuances may differ, so be mindful of the tone and formatting preferences in the Cypriot job market. A well-crafted resume is your passport to the interview stage, so invest time and effort in presenting your professional story effectively.

Preparing for Interviews

Ah, the exhilarating and nerve-wracking moment – the job interview. As you prepare to showcase your skills and personality, consider these tips for navigating interviews in the Cypriot context:

1. **Research the Company:** Demonstrate your genuine interest in the company by researching its history, values, and recent achievements. This knowledge will set you apart and show that you've invested time in understanding your potential workplace.

2. **Understand Cypriot Work Culture:** Familiarize yourself

with the work culture in Cyprus. The pace may be more relaxed than in some other countries, and interpersonal relationships often play a significant role. Showcase your adaptability and collaborative spirit during the interview.

3. **Emphasize Soft Skills:** While technical skills are crucial, Cypriot employers often value soft skills such as teamwork, communication, and adaptability. Share examples of how you've effectively collaborated with diverse teams or navigated challenges with a positive mindset.

4. **Discuss Cultural Integration:** If you're an expatriate, discuss your enthusiasm for cultural integration. Highlight experiences where you've successfully adapted to new environments and embraced diverse cultures. Employers appreciate candidates who bring a global perspective to the workplace.

5. **Ask Thoughtful Questions:** Prepare thoughtful questions to ask the interviewer. This not only demonstrates your genuine interest but also provides insights into the company culture and expectations. Questions about team dynamics, growth opportunities, and the company's vision can be impactful.

Understanding Work Permits and Visas

As you delve into the job market, it's essential to navigate the legal aspects of employment in Cyprus. Work permits and visas are prerequisites for working legally on the island.

For European Union (EU) citizens, the process is relatively straightforward, thanks to the free movement agreements within the EU. Non-EU citizens may need to obtain a work permit, and the type of permit required depends on factors such as the nature of employment, duration, and qualifications.

Consult with the Cypriot embassy or consulate to understand the specific requirements based on your situation. Your prospective employer may also assist you in the application process, guiding you through the necessary steps to ensure compliance with local regulations.

Freelancing and Remote Work Opportunities

In the evolving landscape of work, freelancing and remote opportunities have become increasingly prevalent. If you possess skills that lend themselves to remote work, or if you're considering freelancing, explore platforms that connect professionals with global opportunities.

Websites like Upwork, Freelancer, and Toptal offer a plethora of projects across various industries. Leverage your expertise, create a compelling online profile, and explore the flexibility of working remotely while enjoying the charms of Cyprus.

Dealing with Challenges and Celebrating Success

The job search journey may come with its share of challenges – from navigating cultural differences to overcoming potential language barriers. It's essential to approach challenges with resilience and view them as opportunities for growth.

Embrace the moments of success along the way – the first interview, the positive feedback from a potential employer, and the eventual job offer. Celebrate each milestone, for the job market is not just a terrain of challenges; it's a canvas where you paint the strokes of your professional triumphs.

Chapter in Review

As we wrap up our exploration of navigating the job market in Cyprus, reflect on the steps you've taken to carve out your professional path on the island. From understanding the professional landscape to crafting a compelling resume, acing interviews, and navigating the legal aspects of employment – each step is a brushstroke on the canvas of your Cypriot career adventure.

Remember that the job market isn't just about finding a position; it's about creating a professional journey that aligns with your aspirations and contributes to the dynamic tapestry of Cyprus's workforce.

With a blend of skills, cultural awareness, and a positive mindset, you're poised to thrive in the professional landscape of this sun-kissed island. Welcome to the world of Cypriot opportunities – may your career adventure be as vibrant as the Mediterranean sunset!

Chapter 5
Education System

Welcome to the enlightening journey through Cyprus's educational landscape, a chapter that unfolds the possibilities for both the young minds in your family and perhaps even for you, as lifelong learning knows no age. Cyprus, with its rich cultural heritage and commitment to education, offers a diverse range of opportunities for learners of all ages. As we embark on this exploration, envision education not just as an academic pursuit but as a gateway to cultural immersion, personal growth, and a deeper connection with the vibrant community of learners on this sun-soaked island.

Overview of the Educational Framework

The Cypriot education system is structured, comprehensive, and tailored to meet the needs of students at various stages of their academic journey. It is influenced by both European and British educational traditions, reflecting the island's historical ties.

The system comprises three main levels:

1. **Primary Education:** Primary education in Cyprus is mandatory and caters to children between the ages of 6 and 12. The curriculum covers a broad range of subjects, including Greek language and literature, mathematics, science, social studies, and physical education. English is introduced as a second language from the first grade, laying the foundation for bilingual proficiency.

2. **Secondary Education:** Following primary education, students enter secondary education, which is divided into two cycles. The first cycle, Gymnasio, spans three years (ages 12-15), and the second cycle, Lyceum, covers three additional years (ages 15-18). During the Lyceum phase, students

choose one of three tracks: General, Technical, or Vocational, based on their interests and career goals.

3. **Higher Education:** Cyprus boasts a burgeoning higher education sector, with universities and institutions offering a diverse range of academic programs. The language of instruction is primarily English, attracting international students from around the world. The island has established itself as an academic hub, fostering a dynamic and multicultural learning environment.

International Schools: A Global Perspective

For expatriate families or those seeking an international educational experience, Cyprus hosts a variety of international schools. These institutions often follow international curricula, such as the International Baccalaureate (IB) or the Cambridge International Examinations (CIE) programs, providing a seamless transition for students moving across borders.

International schools not only offer rigorous academic programs but also emphasize cultural diversity, fostering a global perspective among students. The language of instruction is typically English, and the curriculum is designed to prepare students for further studies at universities worldwide.

Whether you're considering primary, secondary, or higher education, the availability of international schools enhances the educational landscape, catering to the diverse needs of expatriate families and students aspiring to experience a globalized approach to learning.

Exploring Higher Education Opportunities

Cyprus, with its commitment to quality education, has emerged as an attractive destination for higher education. The island is home to several reputable universities and institutions that offer a wide array of undergraduate and postgraduate programs.

1. **Universities:** Cyprus hosts both public and private

universities, each with its unique strengths and specializations. Public universities, such as the University of Cyprus and the Cyprus University of Technology, are known for their academic excellence and research contributions. Private institutions, including the University of Nicosia and Frederick University, offer diverse programs in collaboration with international partners.

2. **Programs and Degrees:** From business and engineering to humanities and sciences, Cyprus's universities cover a broad spectrum of academic disciplines. Many programs are offered in collaboration with renowned international universities, providing students with the opportunity to earn degrees recognized globally.

3. **Language of Instruction:** English is the primary language of instruction in higher education, making Cyprus an accessible destination for international students. The multicultural environment enriches the learning experience, fostering cross-cultural interactions and global perspectives.

4. **Research Opportunities:** Cyprus has made significant strides in research and innovation, with universities actively contributing to advancements in various fields. Students keen on research have access to state-of-the-art facilities and collaborative projects, providing a stimulating academic environment.

5. **Student Life:** Beyond academics, the student life in Cyprus is vibrant and diverse. University campuses host a range of extracurricular activities, cultural events, and student organizations. The island's warm climate and picturesque landscapes create an inviting backdrop for a holistic university experience.

Language Considerations in Education

For those venturing into the Cypriot education system or higher education institutions, language considerations play a pivotal role. Here's a breakdown of the linguistic landscape:

1. **Greek Language:** Greek is the official language of Cyprus, and proficiency in Greek can enhance both academic and daily life experiences. While many educational institutions offer programs in English, learning basic Greek phrases can facilitate interactions and create a deeper connection with the local community.

2. **English Language:** English is widely spoken and used as the primary language of instruction in higher education. Most academic programs, especially at the university level, are conducted in English. This bilingual environment not only eases the transition for international students but also reflects the cosmopolitan nature of the island.

3. **Multilingual Environment:** Cyprus's multicultural environment is reflected in the linguistic diversity of its residents. In addition to Greek and English, you may encounter other languages spoken by the expatriate community. Embracing this multilingual tapestry adds a unique dimension to the educational journey.

Navigating the Admission Process

Whether you're enrolling your child in a local school or pursuing higher education for yourself, navigating the admission process is a significant step. Here are some key considerations:

1. **Local Schools:** For primary and secondary education, the admission process typically involves registering your child at the local school in your catchment area. The Ministry of Education and Culture provides guidelines and support for enrollment. Familiarize yourself with the required

documents, application deadlines, and any additional assessments or interviews.

2. **International Schools:** Admission to international schools may involve a more comprehensive process, including submission of academic records, entrance exams, and interviews. Contact the admissions office of your chosen school to gather information on specific requirements and procedures.

3. **Higher Education:** The admission process for higher education varies by institution and program. Most universities have dedicated admissions offices that guide prospective students through the application process. Prepare essential documents, including academic transcripts, letters of recommendation, and a personal statement, and ensure that you meet the specified criteria for your chosen program.

4. **Language Proficiency:** Demonstrating proficiency in the language of instruction is often a requirement for admission to higher education programs. Universities may require standardized test scores, such as the TOEFL or IELTS, as part of the application.

5. **Visa and Residency:** International students pursuing higher education in Cyprus need to consider visa and residency requirements. Check with the relevant authorities and your chosen institution for guidance on obtaining the necessary permits for studying in Cyprus.

Financial Considerations and Scholarships

Education, while invaluable, often comes with financial considerations. As you embark on this educational journey in Cyprus, consider the following:

1. **Tuition Fees:** Tuition fees for higher education programs vary by institution, program, and level of study. Research the

fees associated with your chosen program and factor them into your budget.

2. **Living Expenses:** Beyond tuition, consider the cost of living in Cyprus. This includes accommodation, food, transportation, and other daily expenses. Create a comprehensive budget to ensure that you have a clear understanding of your financial commitments.

3. **Scholarships and Financial Aid:** Explore scholarship opportunities and financial aid options offered by universities, government programs, and private organizations. Scholarships may be merit-based, need-based, or tied to specific fields of study. Research and apply for scholarships that align with your academic achievements and aspirations.

4. **Part-Time Work:** International students in Cyprus are often allowed to work part-time during their studies. Check the regulations and explore part-time work opportunities to supplement your finances and gain valuable work experience.

5. **Budgeting:** Develop a realistic budget that considers both tuition and living expenses. Factor in potential fluctuations in currency exchange rates, and explore cost-saving measures, such as shared accommodation and student discounts.

Cultural Immersion through Education

Education in Cyprus is not just about academic pursuits; it's a gateway to cultural immersion and a deeper understanding of the island's rich heritage. Here are ways to embrace the cultural aspect of your educational journey:

1. **Language Learning:** Engage in language learning to enhance your cultural integration. While English is widely spoken, learning basic Greek phrases can enrich your interactions with locals and deepen your connection with the community.

2. **Participate in Cultural Events:** Attend cultural events,

festivals, and exhibitions to experience the vibrancy of Cypriot culture. From traditional music and dance performances to art exhibitions and literary festivals, the island offers a diverse array of cultural experiences.

3. **Explore Historical Sites:** Cyprus is a treasure trove of historical and archaeological sites. Plan excursions to explore ancient ruins, Byzantine churches, and archaeological museums. Each site tells a story of the island's rich history and cultural evolution.

4. **Connect with Local Communities:** Join local clubs, community groups, or volunteer organizations to connect with Cypriots and fellow expatriates. Engaging in community activities provides insights into daily life, fosters friendships, and broadens your cultural perspective.

5. **Culinary Exploration:** The Cypriot culinary scene is a delightful journey in itself. Explore local markets, savor traditional dishes, and engage in culinary experiences that reflect the island's gastronomic heritage. Food, after all, is a cultural ambassador.

Challenges and Celebrations on the Educational Journey

As with any significant life transition, the educational journey in Cyprus may present its share of challenges and celebrations. Here's how to navigate both:

1. **Cultural Adjustment:** Adjusting to a new educational system, language, and cultural nuances may initially pose challenges. Approach this adjustment with an open mind, seek support from fellow students and educators, and view it as an opportunity for personal growth.

2. **Academic Rigor:** The academic rigor of higher education programs may require adaptation. Develop effective study habits, utilize support services offered by universities, and

don't hesitate to seek guidance from professors or academic advisors.

3. **Building Connections:** Building social connections is an integral part of the educational journey. Attend orientation events, join clubs or student organizations, and actively participate in campus life to foster friendships and create a sense of belonging.

4. **Celebrating Achievements:** Celebrate your academic achievements, no matter how small. From acing an exam to completing a challenging project, each milestone contributes to your educational journey. Acknowledge your efforts and take pride in your accomplishments.

5. **Navigating Setbacks:** Setbacks are a natural part of any educational journey. Whether facing academic challenges or personal obstacles, approach setbacks with resilience. Seek support from professors, classmates, or counseling services to navigate challenges effectively.

Chapter in Review

As we conclude our exploration of the education system in Cyprus, reflect on the educational journey that awaits you or your family. From primary and secondary education to the vibrant higher education landscape, Cyprus offers a spectrum of opportunities for intellectual growth, cultural immersion, and personal development.

Education is not just about acquiring knowledge; it's a transformative journey that shapes perspectives, builds connections, and contributes to the rich tapestry of life experiences. As you step into this chapter of the Cypriot adventure, embrace the joy of learning, celebrate the diversity of educational opportunities, and let the quest for knowledge unfold in harmony with the sunlit landscapes of Cyprus. Welcome to the world of discovery and lifelong learning!

Chapter 6
Healthcare in Cyprus

Ah, the delicate dance between well-being and adventure – a vital aspect of any expatriate journey. Cyprus, with its sun-kissed landscapes and warm embrace, extends not only a haven for the soul but also a commitment to ensuring the health and wellness of its residents. In this chapter, let's unravel the tapestry of healthcare in Cyprus, exploring the medical landscape, navigating healthcare systems, and weaving a narrative of well-being against the backdrop of this Mediterranean gem.

A Prelude to Cypriot Healthcare

Before we delve into the intricacies of healthcare in Cyprus, let's set the stage with a glimpse into the island's commitment to well-being. Cyprus, with its robust healthcare infrastructure, modern medical facilities, and a cadre of skilled healthcare professionals, offers a reassuring environment for residents and visitors alike.

The healthcare system in Cyprus is shaped by a blend of public and private entities, reflecting the island's dedication to providing accessible and high-quality medical care. Whether you're seeking routine check-ups, specialized treatments, or emergency care, Cyprus endeavors to meet your health needs with a touch of warmth and efficiency.

Public Healthcare in Cyprus

The public healthcare system in Cyprus is overseen by the Ministry of Health, and its primary aim is to provide affordable and accessible healthcare services to residents. Contributions to the system are mandatory for those employed in Cyprus, with employers and employees sharing the cost. Expatriates and retirees may also be eligible to participate in the public healthcare system by making voluntary contributions.

Public healthcare services are provided through the General Healthcare System (GHS), which was introduced to enhance the quality and accessibility of medical care. The GHS covers a wide range of medical services, including doctor visits, hospital care, laboratory tests, and prescription medications. Participating in the public healthcare system ensures that residents have access to essential healthcare services at affordable rates.

Private Healthcare: A Tapestry of Choice

In addition to the public healthcare system, Cyprus boasts a thriving private healthcare sector that caters to those seeking personalized and expedited medical services. Private healthcare facilities, including hospitals, clinics, and specialized medical centers, offer a spectrum of services ranging from routine health check-ups to advanced medical treatments.

One of the advantages of private healthcare in Cyprus is the flexibility and choice it affords to individuals. Residents and visitors can opt for private health insurance, which provides access to a network of private healthcare providers. This choice allows individuals to select their preferred doctors, schedule appointments at their convenience, and enjoy personalized medical care tailored to their needs.

Private healthcare facilities in Cyprus often feature state-of-the-art equipment, modern amenities, and a cadre of internationally trained medical professionals. The emphasis on patient-centered care and efficiency contributes to the appeal of private healthcare for those seeking a more personalized and expedited healthcare experience.

Navigating Healthcare Services: A Practical Guide

As you embark on your Cypriot adventure, it's essential to navigate healthcare services with a blend of preparedness and open-mindedness. Here's a practical guide to help you navigate the healthcare landscape in Cyprus:

1. **Public Healthcare Enrollment:** If you're employed in Cyprus, you will likely be automatically enrolled in the public healthcare system, with contributions deducted from your

salary. Expatriates and retirees may voluntarily join the system by submitting the necessary documentation and making the required contributions.

2. **Private Health Insurance:** Consider obtaining private health insurance to complement your healthcare coverage. Private insurance provides additional flexibility, allowing you to choose private healthcare providers and access a broader range of medical services. Compare insurance plans, coverage options, and premiums to find a policy that aligns with your needs.

3. **Doctor Visits:** In Cyprus, you have the choice of consulting with doctors in both the public and private sectors. If you're enrolled in the public healthcare system, you can visit a state doctor without additional charges. For private healthcare, schedule appointments directly with private practitioners based on your preferences and healthcare needs.

4. **Prescription Medications:** Prescription medications are available through both public and private healthcare providers. If you're enrolled in the public healthcare system, prescription medications are subsidized, making them more affordable. Private healthcare may involve out-of-pocket expenses for medications, depending on your insurance coverage.

5. **Emergency Care:** In case of emergencies, Cyprus provides prompt and efficient emergency medical services. Both public and private hospitals have dedicated emergency departments, and ambulance services are accessible throughout the island. Familiarize yourself with the contact numbers for emergency services, including ambulance and medical helplines.

6. **Specialized Care:** For specialized medical care or elective procedures, private healthcare facilities often offer shorter

waiting times and a broader range of services. Research and choose a reputable healthcare provider based on your specific medical needs.

The Multilingual Tapestry of Healthcare

In the mosaic of Cyprus's healthcare landscape, language is a bridge that connects patients and healthcare providers. English is widely spoken in both public and private healthcare settings, making medical consultations, discussions, and explanations accessible to expatriates and international visitors.

Healthcare professionals in Cyprus are often multilingual, and many have received training and education in English-speaking countries. This linguistic diversity contributes to a patient-friendly environment, where clear communication and understanding are paramount.

For those who are more comfortable communicating in other languages, especially in the expatriate community, you may find healthcare providers who speak languages such as Russian, French, or German. Cyprus's multicultural fabric is reflected not only in its landscapes but also in the linguistic tapestry of its healthcare settings.

Wellness and Lifestyle: A Cypriot Perspective

Beyond the clinical aspects of healthcare, Cyprus places a strong emphasis on wellness and a balanced lifestyle. The island's Mediterranean climate, healthy cuisine, and outdoor recreational opportunities contribute to a holistic approach to well-being.

1. **Healthy Cuisine:** The Mediterranean diet, known for its emphasis on fresh fruits, vegetables, olive oil, and lean proteins, is a cornerstone of Cypriot cuisine. Embrace the local culinary delights that contribute to a healthy lifestyle, and savor the flavors of dishes rich in nutrients and antioxidants.

2. **Outdoor Activities:** Cyprus's diverse landscapes offer a playground for outdoor enthusiasts. From hiking trails in the

Troodos Mountains to water sports along the coastline, the island invites you to engage in physical activities that promote fitness and well-being.

3. **Cultural Traditions:** Embrace Cypriot cultural traditions that contribute to well-being, such as communal activities and social gatherings. Participate in local festivals, enjoy the camaraderie of community events, and savor the joyous moments that come with connecting with others.

4. **Sunshine and Vitamin D:** Cyprus's abundant sunshine not only brightens the landscapes but also provides an opportunity for natural vitamin D intake. Enjoy outdoor activities, bask in the sunlight, and relish the benefits of a climate that nurtures both the body and the spirit.

5. **Relaxation and Mindfulness:** The laid-back pace of life in Cyprus offers opportunities for relaxation and mindfulness. Whether it's a leisurely stroll along the coastline, moments of reflection in historic surroundings, or indulging in spa experiences, Cyprus provides a conducive environment for rejuvenation.

Challenges and Solutions in Healthcare

As with any healthcare system, challenges may arise, and it's essential to approach them with a proactive mindset. Here are common challenges and potential solutions in navigating healthcare in Cyprus:

1. **Language Barriers:** While English is widely spoken, language barriers may still pose challenges, especially in rural areas. To overcome this, consider learning basic Greek phrases to enhance communication. Language learning apps and local language classes can be valuable resources.

2. **Waiting Times:** In the public healthcare system, waiting times for non-emergency procedures may be longer. Private healthcare options often offer shorter waiting times,

providing an alternative for those seeking expedited medical services.

3. **Insurance Coverage:** Understanding the terms and conditions of your health insurance coverage is crucial. Be aware of the services covered, co-payment requirements, and any exclusions. Consult with your insurance provider to clarify any uncertainties and ensure comprehensive coverage.

4. **Access to Specialists:** Access to specialized medical care may require referrals in the public healthcare system. Private healthcare often provides more direct access to specialists. Research the availability of specialists in your area and explore options based on your medical needs.

5. **Integration with Public and Private Services:** For those utilizing both public and private healthcare services, maintaining seamless integration can be a challenge. Keep organized records of medical history, test results, and prescriptions to facilitate smooth transitions between different healthcare providers.

Celebrating Health and Well-being in Cyprus

As you navigate the intricate threads of healthcare in Cyprus, take a moment to celebrate the inherent joy of well-being. From the warmth of the Mediterranean sun to the embrace of a healthcare system committed to your health, Cyprus offers a holistic environment that nurtures both body and spirit.

Celebrate the moments of wellness – the invigorating walks along the coastline, the laughter shared with friends over a healthy meal, and the assurance that in Cyprus, your well-being is woven into the fabric of daily life. Approach healthcare not just as a necessity but as a harmonious dance with life's rhythms, guided by the gentle breezes and sunlit landscapes of this enchanting island.

Chapter in Review

As we conclude our exploration of healthcare in Cyprus, reflect on the layers of well-being that await you. From the public healthcare system's embrace of accessibility to the personalized choices offered by private healthcare, Cyprus beckons you to prioritize your health in a landscape that seamlessly blends modernity with tradition.

Healthcare in Cyprus is more than a clinical experience; it's an invitation to embrace a lifestyle that prioritizes balance, nourishment, and the joy of living. As you step into this chapter of the Cypriot journey, may your health and well-being be woven into the vibrant tapestry of life on this sun-drenched island. Here's to the journey of thriving and celebrating the gift of health in the heart of the Mediterranean. Welcome to the sanctuary of well-being – welcome to Cyprus!

Chapter 7
Financial Considerations

Ah, the dance of numbers, the rhythm of currencies, and the melody of financial decisions – welcome to the symphony of financial considerations in the enchanting world of Cyprus. As you embark on your Cypriot adventure, whether for a short stay or a more extended rendezvous, navigating the financial landscape is a crucial step towards a harmonious and worry-free experience. Join me as we explore the monetary nuances, banking ballets, and the delightful choreography of managing your finances on this Mediterranean stage.

Currency Rhapsody: The Euro's Waltz

In the heart of Cyprus, the Euro takes center stage, and its melodious presence permeates every transaction, from the local markets to the charming cafes that dot the streets. The Euro, abbreviated as EUR, is the official currency of the Republic of Cyprus, bringing a harmonious unity to the island's financial landscape.

As you waltz into the world of Cypriot finances, acquaint yourself with the Euro's tempo. Familiarize yourself with the various denominations of banknotes and coins, from the graceful 5 Euro note to the regal 500 Euro note. The Euro, with its intricate design and representation of European heritage, is not just a means of exchange but a cultural emblem that adds a touch of continental charm to your financial transactions.

Banking Ballet: Opening an Account

The first pirouette in your financial ballet involves opening a bank account in Cyprus. Whether you're a resident, an expatriate, or a visitor planning an extended stay, having a local bank account is key to seamlessly managing your finances. The banks in Cyprus offer a range of services, and each financial institution adds its own flair to the banking experience.

1. **Research and Choose a Bank:** Cyprus is home to a variety of banks, both local and international. Research the options, compare the services offered, and choose a bank that aligns with your financial needs. Consider factors such as account fees, accessibility of ATMs, and online banking facilities.

2. **Required Documents:** The choreography of opening a bank account requires a set of documents. Assemble the necessary paperwork, including proof of identity (passport or national ID), proof of address (utility bills or rental agreement), and proof of income or employment. Non-residents may need additional documentation, so check with your chosen bank for specific requirements.

3. **In-Person or Online:** Many banks in Cyprus offer the convenience of online account opening, allowing you to initiate the process from the comfort of your home. Alternatively, you can visit a branch in person to complete the account opening procedure. Choose the method that suits your preferences and schedule.

4. **Currency Accounts:** Consider opening both Euro and foreign currency accounts, especially if you receive income or have expenses in multiple currencies. Having the flexibility to manage different currencies within the same banking platform can simplify financial transactions and enhance convenience.

5. **Debit and Credit Cards:** Your bank account in Cyprus often comes with a debit card, offering a convenient way to make purchases and withdraw cash. Explore the option of obtaining a credit card for additional flexibility. Check the card fees, usage limits, and any associated benefits.

Budgeting Pas de Deux: Managing Your Finances

With your bank account in place, the next movement in our financial ballet involves the art of budgeting. Whether you're a meticulous planner or a free-spirited spender, having a budget is the compass that guides your financial journey in Cyprus.

1. **Income and Expenses:** Begin by mapping out your sources of income and anticipated expenses. This may include salary, rental income, or any other financial inflows. List your regular expenses, such as rent or mortgage payments, utilities, groceries, transportation, and entertainment.

2. **Emergency Fund:** In the choreography of financial well-being, the emergency fund performs a vital role. Set aside a portion of your income into a dedicated savings account to cover unforeseen expenses or emergencies. This financial safety net provides peace of mind and ensures you're prepared for unexpected twists in life's performance.

3. **Currency Exchange Planning:** If you're managing multiple currencies, plan your currency exchanges strategically. Monitor exchange rates and consider converting funds when the rates are favorable. Some banks offer tools or services that allow you to lock in rates for future transactions.

4. **Automate Your Finances:** Embrace the convenience of automation. Set up automatic transfers for savings, bill payments, and other recurring expenses. Automation ensures that your financial commitments are met on time, allowing you to focus on the more enjoyable aspects of your Cypriot adventure.

5. **Financial Goals:** Envision your financial goals – whether it's saving for a dream vacation, investing in personal development, or building a nest egg for the future. Establish short-term and long-term financial goals, and create a roadmap to achieve them. Celebrate your financial

achievements along the way.

Local Rhythms: Cost of Living in Cyprus

As you waltz through your Cypriot journey, it's essential to attune yourself to the local rhythms of the cost of living. Cyprus, with its diverse landscapes and cultural offerings, brings with it a unique set of financial considerations that shape your day-to-day experiences.

1. **Accommodation Costs:** The cost of accommodation varies based on factors such as location, property type, and amenities. Explore rental options, consider shared accommodations if applicable, and factor in utilities and maintenance costs.

2. **Groceries and Dining:** The local markets in Cyprus offer a delightful array of fresh produce, cheeses, and Mediterranean delights. Dining out, whether in traditional tavernas or international restaurants, contributes to the culinary journey. Compare prices, explore local markets, and balance dining out with cooking at home to manage food expenses.

3. **Transportation Expenses:** Cyprus, with its scenic landscapes, invites exploration. Consider transportation costs, including fuel, public transportation fares, or vehicle maintenance if you own a car. Cyprus's compact size also makes cycling or walking viable options in certain areas.

4. **Utilities and Communications:** Budget for utilities such as electricity, water, and internet services. Explore mobile phone plans and internet packages to find options that align with your communication needs.

5. **Entertainment and Recreation:** The cultural tapestry of Cyprus includes a vibrant array of entertainment options, from music festivals to outdoor activities. Plan for entertainment and recreational expenses, and explore local events and activities that align with your interests.

Taxation Tango: Understanding Tax Obligations

In the financial dance of living in Cyprus, understanding your tax obligations is a crucial step. Cyprus, with its favorable tax environment, attracts individuals seeking a tax-efficient destination. Here's a brief overview of key tax considerations:

1. **Residency and Taxation:** Your tax obligations in Cyprus are linked to your residency status. Residents are taxed on their worldwide income, while non-residents are taxed only on income earned in Cyprus. Understanding your residency status is fundamental to determining your tax liabilities.

2. **Personal Income Tax:** Cyprus operates on a progressive income tax system, with tax rates that vary based on income levels. Familiarize yourself with the applicable tax brackets and rates to plan your financial affairs effectively.

3. **Double Taxation Treaties:** Cyprus has an extensive network of double taxation treaties with numerous countries, aiming to prevent double taxation on income. If you're an expatriate or have financial ties to another country, explore the double taxation treaty that may apply to you.

4. **Property Taxes:** Property owners in Cyprus are subject to various property taxes, including immovable property tax and capital gains tax on property transactions. If you own or plan to own property, understand the associated tax implications.

5. **Wealth and Inheritance Taxes:** Cyprus does not impose wealth or inheritance taxes. However, if you have assets or inheritance ties to other countries, consider the tax regulations in those jurisdictions.

Expatriate Finale: Navigating Financial Challenges

As an expatriate in Cyprus, you may encounter specific financial challenges that add a unique rhythm to your financial ballet. Addressing these challenges with grace and proactive planning enhances your financial well-being. Here are common expatriate financial considerations:

1. **Currency Fluctuations:** Stay attuned to currency fluctuations, especially if you have income or financial commitments in a different currency. Monitor exchange rates, explore hedging options if applicable, and consider the impact of currency movements on your budget.

2. **Pension Planning:** If you're an expatriate retiree, pension planning is a critical aspect of your financial journey. Understand the tax implications of receiving pensions in Cyprus, explore international pension transfer options, and ensure that your retirement income aligns with your lifestyle.

3. **Health Insurance:** Health insurance is a fundamental aspect of expatriate life. Whether you're covered by the public healthcare system, have private health insurance, or a combination of both, ensure that your health insurance aligns with your healthcare needs and preferences.

4. **Cross-Border Financial Planning:** If you have financial ties to other countries, such as investments, bank accounts, or properties, adopt a cross-border financial planning approach. Consider consulting with financial advisors who specialize in international financial planning to navigate the complexities of cross-border finances.

5. **Legal and Regulatory Compliance:** Expatriates in Cyprus must navigate legal and regulatory compliance, including residency requirements, work permits, and tax obligations. Stay informed about changes in regulations, consult with legal professionals if needed, and ensure that your financial affairs align with local laws.

Financial Well-being: A Celebratory Crescendo

As we approach the final movement of our financial symphony, take a moment to celebrate the crescendo of financial well-being in Cyprus. Your financial journey, guided by the Euro's melody, the banking ballet, and the taxation tango, contributes to the harmonious experience of life on this sun-drenched island.

Celebrate the financial milestones – from opening your first Cypriot bank account to navigating the intricacies of taxation as an expatriate. Embrace the financial rhythms of Cyprus, where financial management becomes a joyful dance rather than a chore.

As you step into the finale of this financial chapter, may your financial well-being be a source of confidence and freedom. The financial dance in Cyprus is not just about numbers; it's a celebration of the opportunities, experiences, and the rich tapestry of life that this Mediterranean jewel offers. Here's to the financial journey – may it be as vibrant and fulfilling as a Cypriot sunset. Welcome to the symphony of financial well-being in Cyprus!

Chapter 8
Language and Communication

Welcome to the poetic symphony of words and the intricate dance of communication in the captivating embrace of Cyprus. In this chapter, we explore the linguistic landscape of the island, where languages converge like the gentle waves meeting the shore. Whether you're a seasoned traveler or a newcomer to Cypriot shores, understanding the nuances of language and communication adds a rich layer to your journey, connecting you with the heart and soul of this Mediterranean gem.

The Melody of Languages: A Linguistic Tapestry

Cyprus, with its vibrant history and multicultural influences, boasts a linguistic tapestry that reflects the island's diverse heritage. The official languages of Cyprus are Greek and Turkish, a reflection of the island's complex political and historical background. This bilingual character, unique to Cyprus, adds a distinctive flavor to daily life, creating a harmonious coexistence of languages.

1. **Greek Language:** Greek is the predominant language spoken in the Republic of Cyprus, encompassing the southern and western parts of the island. The melodious tones of Greek echo through conversations, marketplaces, and the labyrinthine streets of Cypriot towns. As you navigate the landscapes, familiarizing yourself with basic Greek phrases becomes a delightful tool for communication and cultural immersion.

   ◦ **Greetings:** Embrace the warmth of Cypriot hospitality by mastering simple greetings. "Kalimera" signifies "good morning," "Kalispera" is "good evening," and "Kalinikta" bids "good night." These greetings, offered with a genuine smile, open doors to friendly interactions.

- ○ **Common Phrases:** Expand your linguistic repertoire with common phrases. "Efharisto" expresses gratitude, "Parakalo" is used for "please" or "you're welcome," and "Ne" means "yes," while "Ochi" is "no." These phrases, sprinkled into your conversations, evoke appreciation and camaraderie.
- ○ **Navigating Menus:** Exploring Cypriot cuisine is a culinary adventure. Decode menus with ease by learning food-related terms. "Psomi" is bread, "Kreas" means meat, and "Horta" refers to greens. Your culinary escapades become more delightful when flavored with a sprinkle of local language.

2. **Turkish Language:** In the northern part of Cyprus, the Turkish language takes center stage. Turkish, with its lyrical cadence, adds another layer of linguistic charm to the island. While Greek and Turkish are the official languages, English is widely spoken, especially in urban areas and tourist destinations, fostering an inclusive and accessible environment for international visitors.

- ○ **Turkish Greetings:** Extend friendly greetings in Turkish to enrich your interactions. "Merhaba" is "hello," "Günaydın" means "good morning," and "Iyi akşamlar" is "good evening." Simple gestures of linguistic courtesy enhance your connection with the local community.
- ○ **Essential Phrases:** Equip yourself with essential Turkish phrases for daily encounters. "Teşekkür ederim" expresses gratitude, "Lütfen" is "please," and "Evet" means "yes," while "Hayır" signifies "no." These phrases, shared with sincerity, create a bridge

between cultures.

- ○ **Cultural Expressions:** Immerse yourself in the cultural richness of northern Cyprus by learning expressions specific to Turkish customs. "Selam" is a casual greeting, "Hoş geldiniz" means "welcome," and "Güle güle" is used to bid someone farewell with a wish for them to go with a smile.

The Lingua Franca: English in Cyprus

In the grand orchestration of languages, English emerges as the lingua franca that unites diverse communities and facilitates seamless communication. English is widely spoken and understood, especially in urban areas, tourist hotspots, and educational institutions. This linguistic inclusivity creates an inviting environment for international visitors and expatriates, making Cyprus an accessible destination for those who may not be fluent in Greek or Turkish.

1. **English in Everyday Life:** English permeates various facets of daily life in Cyprus. From signage and public announcements to menus and service encounters, the English language extends a welcoming embrace to those exploring the island. This linguistic inclusivity contributes to the ease of navigation for English-speaking travelers.
2. **Business and Education:** English holds a significant presence in the business and education sectors. Many professionals and educators in Cyprus are proficient in English, facilitating communication in work environments and educational institutions. This linguistic diversity enhances the island's appeal for international students and professionals seeking opportunities in Cyprus.
3. **Tourism and Hospitality:** Cyprus, with its allure as a tourist destination, prioritizes English in the tourism and hospitality

sectors. Accommodation providers, tour operators, and service personnel often communicate effectively in English, ensuring that visitors feel at home and can navigate the island with ease.

Cultural Etiquette: The Language of Respect

In the grand ballroom of cross-cultural communication, under-standing and respecting local customs and etiquette are the essential dance partners. Cyprus, with its rich cultural tapestry, has nuances that shape courteous interactions and foster positive connections. Here are key aspects of cultural etiquette in Cyprus:

1. **Greetings and Politeness:** Greetings are a cornerstone of Cypriot culture. When meeting someone, a handshake is a common form of greeting. Address individuals with courtesy titles, such as "Mr." or "Mrs.," until invited to use first names. Expressing gratitude and politeness through phrases like "Efharisto" and "Lütfen" is appreciated.

2. **Socializing:** Cypriots value social connections and warmth in interactions. Engage in conversations with genuine interest, and don't be surprised if personal questions are asked; it's a reflection of the friendly nature of Cypriot culture. When invited to someone's home, it's customary to bring a small gift as a token of appreciation.

3. **Respecting Elders:** Respect for elders is deeply ingrained in Cypriot culture. When interacting with older individuals, use formal titles and demonstrate deference. It's common for younger individuals to offer their seat to older individuals, a gesture of respect that aligns with Cypriot cultural values.

4. **Dress Code:** In more formal settings, a conservative dress code is appreciated. Women often opt for dresses or skirts, while men may wear suits or collared shirts. In casual settings, such as beachside cafes or outdoor markets, comfortable and

modest attire is acceptable.

5. **Tipping Culture:** Tipping is customary in Cyprus, and it's a way to express satisfaction with service. In restaurants, leaving a tip of around 10% is common. Tipping taxi drivers, hotel staff, and other service providers is also appreciated. Check for service charges included in bills, and adjust tipping accordingly.

Navigating Multilingual Conversations: A Social Waltz

As you engage in conversations in the multilingual setting of Cyprus, embracing the art of multilingual communication becomes a valuable skill. Here are tips for navigating conversations seamlessly:

1. **Language Flexibility:** Be flexible in your language use. Cypriots appreciate the effort to communicate in their native languages, even if it's just a few phrases. Switching between Greek, Turkish, and English based on the context fosters a sense of cultural sensitivity.

2. **Language Apps:** Language learning apps can be valuable companions on your linguistic journey. Explore apps that offer Greek and Turkish language lessons to enhance your proficiency and confidence in daily interactions.

3. **Language Exchanges:** Engage in language exchanges with local residents or language partners. Language exchange programs provide opportunities to practice Greek and Turkish while sharing insights into your own language and culture.

4. **Cultural Curiosity:** Cultivate a curiosity for Cypriot culture and expressions. Ask questions about language nuances, regional dialects, and cultural references. Cypriots often appreciate the interest shown in understanding the intricacies of their linguistic and cultural heritage.

5. **Bilingual Events:** Attend bilingual events or language

exchange meet-ups. These gatherings create a platform for practicing both Greek and Turkish, connecting with locals, and building a network of friends who appreciate the beauty of language diversity.

Digital Communication: Navigating the Virtual Seas

In the age of digital connectivity, the virtual seas of communication play a significant role in staying connected and informed. Whether you're communicating with friends, colleagues, or accessing essential services, navigating digital communication adds a modern cadence to your Cypriot experience.

1. **Social Media Platforms:** Social media platforms are vibrant spaces for staying updated on local events, connecting with communities, and accessing information. Many businesses, organizations, and government entities use social media to share updates and communicate with the public.

2. **Messaging Apps:** Messaging apps are popular for both personal and professional communication. WhatsApp and Viber are widely used in Cyprus for text messaging, voice calls, and sharing media. These apps provide convenient channels for staying connected with friends and colleagues.

3. **Online Services:** Embrace the convenience of online services for essential tasks. Whether it's banking, utility payments, or scheduling appointments, many services in Cyprus offer online platforms for streamlined and efficient transactions.

4. **Language Translation Apps:** Language translation apps can be valuable tools for overcoming language barriers in digital communication. Explore apps that support translation between Greek, Turkish, and English to enhance your digital communication experience.

Challenges and Solutions in Multilingual Communication

In the grand ballroom of multilingual communication, challenges may arise, but with a dash of adaptability and cultural understanding, solutions unfold gracefully:

1. **Language Proficiency:** If you're still mastering Greek or Turkish, navigating conversations may pose initial challenges. However, Cypriots are generally patient and understanding, appreciating the effort to engage in their native languages. Continue learning, practice regularly, and celebrate the progress you make.

2. **Dialect Variations:** Regional dialects and accents may vary across Cyprus, adding nuances to the languages spoken. Embrace the diversity of linguistic expressions, and don't hesitate to ask for clarification if you encounter unfamiliar terms or expressions.

3. **Language Mixing:** Cypriots often mix Greek and Turkish words in conversations, creating a linguistic blend known as "Cypriot Greek" or "Cypriot Turkish." Embrace the fluidity of language use, and feel free to ask for explanations if you encounter words or phrases that intrigue you.

4. **Cultural Sensitivity:** Cultural sensitivity is a guiding principle in effective multilingual communication. Be attuned to cultural cues, practice active listening, and approach conversations with an open heart. Understanding the cultural context enriches your language experience and fosters meaningful connections.

5. **Language Support Services:** If you encounter situations where language proficiency becomes a barrier, seek language support services. Many businesses, especially in tourist areas, offer support in English. Additionally, language support services may be available through community centers, language schools, or expatriate networks.

A Multilingual Celebration: Language as a Bridge

As we approach the finale of our exploration into language and communication in Cyprus, let's celebrate the diverse linguistic landscape that adds color to the Cypriot experience. Language, with its power to connect hearts and bridge cultures, becomes a harmonious melody in the symphony of Cypriot life.

In Cyprus, language is not just a means of communication; it's a bridge that connects individuals across cultural divides. Embrace the beauty of linguistic diversity, share in the joy of learning and practicing new phrases, and revel in the richness of conversations that echo with the cadence of Greek, Turkish, and English.

May your linguistic journey in Cyprus be a source of delight, connecting you with the vibrant stories, traditions, and expressions that shape this sun-drenched island. As you engage in the dance of words, may language become a celebration of shared experiences, a bridge that unites, and a testament to the beauty of cultural diversity. Welcome to the multilingual symphony of Cyprus – where every word is a step in the dance of connection and understanding.

Chapter 9
Cultural Integration

Welcome to the heart of the Cypriot experience, where the vibrant tapestry of culture unfolds in every corner, inviting you to dance to the rhythm of traditions, customs, and shared stories. Cultural integration in Cyprus is not a mere assimilation; it's an immersive journey into the soul of an island that wears its cultural heritage with pride. As you embark on this chapter of your Cypriot adventure, prepare to be enchanted by the warmth of hospitality, the richness of traditions, and the harmonious blend of influences that make Cyprus a captivating crossroads of cultures.

The Melting Pot of Cypriot Culture

Picture a potpourri of influences – Greek, Turkish, Phoenician, Roman, Byzantine, Ottoman – all simmering together in the Mediterranean sun, infusing the air with the fragrances of history and heritage. Cypriot culture, like a fine mosaic, is composed of diverse elements that have shaped the island's identity over centuries.

1. **Language and Identity:** Language is a key pillar of cultural identity in Cyprus. The island's bilingual character, with Greek and Turkish as official languages, reflects its historical and political complexities. English, as a widely spoken language, adds a global resonance to the cultural symphony. Engage with locals in their native languages, embrace linguistic nuances, and savor the multilingual charm that defines Cypriot communication.
2. **Religious Harmony:** The echoes of church bells and the calls to prayer weave a tapestry of religious harmony in Cyprus. The majority of the population follows Orthodox Christianity, while there is a significant Muslim community.

Religious festivals, ceremonies, and traditions create a harmonious coexistence, showcasing the island's commitment to diversity and respect for different faiths.

3. **Culinary Kaleidoscope:** Prepare your taste buds for a culinary journey that mirrors Cyprus's diverse cultural influences. From moussaka and souvlaki to kleftiko and halloumi, each dish narrates a story of cultural intermingling. Embrace the art of meze – a delightful array of small dishes – and indulge in the flavors of a cuisine that reflects the island's historical crossroads.

4. **Traditional Arts and Crafts:** Wander through Cypriot villages, and you'll encounter artisans practicing traditional crafts passed down through generations. Lefkaritika lace, basket weaving, and pottery are among the crafts that showcase the island's commitment to preserving its cultural heritage. Engage with local artisans, appreciate their skills, and perhaps take home a piece of Cypriot craftsmanship as a memento.

Cultural Etiquette: Navigating Social Customs

As you immerse yourself in Cypriot culture, understanding social customs and etiquette becomes the compass guiding your interactions. Cultural etiquette in Cyprus reflects the island's warm and sociable nature. Here are insights into key aspects of Cypriot social customs:

1. **Hospitality as a Virtue:** Hospitality is ingrained in Cypriot culture, and guests are treated with genuine warmth. When invited to someone's home, it's customary to bring a small gift as a token of appreciation. The host will likely insist on serving ample food and drinks, so embrace the generosity and savor the culinary delights offered.

2. **Respect for Elders:** Respect for elders is a cornerstone of Cypriot values. When interacting with older individuals, use

formal titles and demonstrate deference. It's common for younger individuals to offer their seat to older individuals, a gesture rooted in respect for age and experience.

3. **Socializing and Small Talk:** Cypriots value social connections, and engaging in friendly small talk is a common practice. Expect personal questions as an expression of genuine interest rather than intrusion. Be open to sharing aspects of your own life, as reciprocal sharing is a part of building meaningful connections.

4. **Celebrating Festivals:** Cyprus is a land of festivals, each one a celebration of cultural, religious, or historical significance. Participate in local festivals, join in the festivities, and experience the joyous atmosphere that permeates the streets. From the colorful Carnival to the solemn Easter celebrations, each festival unveils a different facet of Cypriot culture.

5. **Dress Code:** While Cypriot society is generally casual and relaxed, there are occasions that call for a more formal dress code. In religious settings or formal events, dressing modestly is appreciated. When in doubt, opt for conservative attire to show respect for cultural norms.

Experiencing Cypriot Traditions: A Cultural Odyssey

The heartbeat of Cypriot culture is felt most profoundly through its traditions – age-old customs that have withstood the test of time and continue to resonate in daily life. Let's embark on a cultural odyssey, exploring traditions that add depth to your integration into Cypriot life.

1. **Cyprus Meze Experience:** Meze is not just a culinary delight; it's a social and cultural experience. Gather with friends or family at a traditional taverna and savor the communal joy of sharing small plates of flavorful dishes. From olives and hummus to grilled meats and seafood, each

meze item contributes to a symphony of tastes.

2. **Kopiaste – The Invitation:** "Kopiaste" means "come and join us" in Greek, and it encapsulates the spirit of Cypriot hospitality. Whether uttered by a friend or a stranger, this invitation embodies the welcoming nature of Cypriot culture. Respond with a smile and an open heart, and you'll find yourself embraced by the warmth of Cypriot camaraderie.

3. **Weddings and Celebrations:** Cypriot weddings are grand celebrations that fuse tradition with joyous revelry. If you have the opportunity to attend a Cypriot wedding, you'll witness lively music, elaborate ceremonies, and a feast that reflects the island's commitment to celebrating life's milestones with gusto. Participate with enthusiasm, and you'll be part of a cherished cultural experience.

4. **Olive Harvest Festivities:** The olive tree, an emblem of Cyprus, takes center stage during the annual olive harvest. If you find yourself on the island during this season, consider joining local communities in olive-picking activities. It's not just about harvesting olives; it's a communal gathering that underscores the cultural significance of this timeless tradition.

5. **Cypriot Coffee Ritual:** Coffee, in Cyprus, is not just a beverage; it's a ritual that unfolds with grace and ceremony. Participate in the Cypriot coffee culture by sipping on a strong and aromatic cup of traditional coffee. Engage in conversation, share stories, and savor the flavors of a beverage that symbolizes Cypriot sociability.

Cross-Cultural Connections: Embracing Diversity

Cultural integration in Cyprus goes beyond mere adaptation; it's about embracing diversity and building cross-cultural connections. The island's cosmopolitan atmosphere, shaped by centuries of influences, invites you to engage with a mosaic of cultures and perspectives. Here are ways to foster cross-cultural connections in Cyprus:

1. **Attend Cultural Events:** Cyprus hosts a myriad of cultural events, from music festivals to art exhibitions. Attend these events to immerse yourself in the creative expressions of diverse communities. Engaging with cultural activities provides opportunities to connect with locals who share a passion for the arts.

2. **Language Exchange Programs:** Participate in language exchange programs to connect with local residents and language partners. Language exchanges not only enhance your linguistic skills but also foster cultural understanding. Learning about each other's languages and customs becomes a shared journey of discovery.

3. **Community Involvement:** Get involved in community initiatives and volunteer opportunities. Whether it's participating in local clean-up events, supporting charitable organizations, or contributing to cultural preservation projects, community involvement opens doors to meaningful connections with like-minded individuals.

4. **Explore Multicultural Neighborhoods:** Cyprus is home to multicultural neighborhoods where diverse communities coexist. Explore these areas, engage with residents, and discover the cultural gems that contribute to the mosaic of Cypriot life. Share in the vibrancy of cultural diversity through culinary adventures, festivals, and community gatherings.

5. **Join Expat Networks:** If you're an expatriate in Cyprus, join expat networks and social groups. Expat communities provide a supportive environment where individuals from different cultural backgrounds share their experiences, offer

advice, and build lasting friendships. Attend expat meet-ups to connect with fellow expatriates and locals alike.

Navigating Cultural Differences: A Compassionate Approach

In the realm of cultural integration, navigating cultural differences with compassion and openness is key to building harmonious connections. Cyprus, with its diverse cultural landscape, invites you to approach cultural differences with curiosity rather than judgment. Here are guiding principles for navigating cultural differences:

1. **Cultural Sensitivity:** Cultivate cultural sensitivity by being attuned to the traditions, customs, and values of different communities in Cyprus. Recognize that practices may vary across regions and among individuals. Approach cultural differences with an open mind and a willingness to learn.

2. **Active Listening:** Practice active listening in cultural exchanges. Take the time to understand different perspectives, ask questions with genuine curiosity, and appreciate the richness that cultural diversity adds to the tapestry of Cypriot life. Listening becomes a bridge that fosters understanding and connection.

3. **Seek Understanding:** When encountering cultural differences, seek understanding rather than making assumptions. If you have questions or find certain customs unfamiliar, don't hesitate to ask for explanations. Cypriots often appreciate the interest shown in their cultural heritage and are happy to share insights.

4. **Participate with Respect:** When engaging in cultural traditions or celebrations, participate with respect for the significance of each practice. Whether attending religious ceremonies, festivals, or family gatherings, your respectful participation enhances the sense of unity and shared experiences.

5. **Embrace Adaptability:** Cultural integration is a dynamic process that involves adaptation and flexibility. Embrace the ebb and flow of cultural experiences, and be open to adapting certain aspects of your own behavior to align with cultural norms. Flexibility fosters a sense of belonging and mutual understanding.

Celebrating Cultural Integration: A Shared Symphony

As we approach the final movement of our exploration into cultural integration in Cyprus, let's celebrate the shared symphony that emerges when diverse cultures converge. Cultural integration is not about erasing differences; it's about finding harmony in diversity, celebrating the beauty of varied perspectives, and weaving a tapestry that reflects the collective spirit of a community.

In Cyprus, cultural integration is an ongoing dance, a continual dialogue between traditions old and new, between communities with rich histories and individuals forging new connections. As you navigate the cultural landscape of Cyprus, may your journey be marked by moments of shared laughter, the warmth of hospitality, and the discovery of common threads that bind us all.

Welcome to the celebration of cultural integration in Cyprus – where every step, every gesture, and every shared experience contributes to the rich narrative of a community that thrives on the beauty of diversity. May your own cultural journey in Cyprus be a source of enrichment, connection, and the joyous discovery of the shared humanity that unites us all.

Chapter 10
Transportation in Cyprus

Picture yourself on the sun-kissed shores of Cyprus, where the azure waters beckon and the ancient landscapes whisper tales of history. As you embark on your Cypriot adventure, navigating the island's transportation networks becomes a vital rhythm in the symphony of exploration. From the winding roads that unveil scenic vistas to the bustling urban hubs pulsating with life, this chapter is your guide to the diverse modes of transportation that weave through the fabric of Cyprus.

The Dance of Roads: Driving in Cyprus

Feel the thrill of the open road beneath your wheels as you navigate Cyprus by car. Driving is one of the most popular and flexible ways to explore the island, offering the freedom to chart your own course and uncover hidden gems along the way.

1. **Driving Culture:** Cyprus follows the left-hand driving system, a legacy of its British colonial history. The road network is well-maintained, featuring modern highways, scenic coastal routes, and charming mountain roads. While urban areas may have busy traffic, especially during peak hours, the overall driving culture is relaxed, and road trips are embraced as a quintessential Cypriot experience.

2. **Renting a Car:** Renting a car is a convenient option for travelers who prefer flexibility in their explorations. Numerous car rental agencies operate across the island, offering a range of vehicles from compact cars to rugged SUVs. Ensure you have a valid driver's license and familiarize yourself with local traffic rules before embarking on your Cypriot road adventure.

3. **Scenic Routes:** The allure of Cyprus lies not just in its

destinations but in the journey itself. Explore the scenic routes that crisscross the island, each offering a unique panorama of landscapes. From the coastal drive between Paphos and Limassol to the mountainous trails leading to Troodos, every road is an invitation to savor the diverse beauty of Cyprus.

4. **Traffic and Parking:** While urban areas may experience congestion during rush hours, traffic is generally manageable. Parking facilities are available in towns and cities, often marked with blue lines indicating paid parking areas. Pay attention to parking signs and regulations to avoid fines, and enjoy the convenience of exploring both urban centers and rural landscapes at your own pace.

5. **Public Transportation:** Public transportation is also a viable option for those who prefer to leave the driving to others. Buses connect major cities and towns, offering an affordable and efficient means of getting around. Intercity buses are equipped with air conditioning, making the journey comfortable even during the warmer months.

Navigating the Seas: Ferry Adventures

As an island in the Mediterranean, Cyprus invites you to explore its maritime beauty through ferry adventures. Whether you're hopping between coastal towns or setting sail to nearby islands, ferry travel adds a nautical charm to your Cypriot experience.

1. **Interconnected Ports:** Cyprus boasts well-connected ports that facilitate ferry services between the island's coastal towns and beyond. Limassol, Larnaca, and Paphos are key hubs for ferry departures, offering travelers the chance to embark on sea journeys to destinations such as Greece, Israel, and other neighboring islands.

2. **Island-Hopping:** Embrace the spirit of island-hopping by

boarding ferries to nearby gems like Akamas Peninsula or the stunning Blue Lagoon. These shorter ferry rides provide an opportunity to witness the coastal beauty of Cyprus from a different perspective and add a maritime rhythm to your itinerary.

3. **Cruises and Boat Tours:** For a leisurely exploration of the coastline, consider joining a cruise or boat tour. Numerous operators offer excursions, ranging from sunset cruises to full-day sailing adventures. Cruise along the crystal-clear waters, discover hidden coves, and bask in the Mediterranean sun as you create maritime memories.

4. **Traveling to Northern Cyprus:** If you wish to explore the northern part of the island, you can cross the border from the Republic of Cyprus to Northern Cyprus. However, it's essential to check the latest regulations and border crossing requirements. Once in Northern Cyprus, you can continue your journey by car or public transportation.

Wings to Soar: Air Travel in Cyprus

For those seeking swift and efficient travel between cities or wishing to arrive quickly from abroad, air travel becomes the wings to soar across the Cypriot skies. Cyprus boasts international airports that cater to both domestic and international flights.

1. **Larnaca International Airport:** Serving as the main international gateway, Larnaca International Airport welcomes flights from major cities across Europe, the Middle East, and beyond. The airport is equipped with modern facilities, including duty-free shops, lounges, and car rental services. Whether you're arriving or departing, the airport offers a seamless travel experience.

2. **Paphos International Airport:** Paphos International Airport, located on the western coast of Cyprus, is another

key entry point for travelers. It handles both domestic and international flights, providing convenient access to popular destinations in the Paphos region.

3. **Domestic Flights:** While Cyprus is a relatively small island, domestic flights are available for those looking to reduce travel time between cities. These flights connect Larnaca and Paphos, offering a quick and efficient mode of transportation for business or leisure travelers.

4. **Airport Transfers:** Upon arrival, transportation options from the airports include taxis, car rentals, and shuttle services. Taxis are readily available outside the airport terminals, providing a convenient and direct transfer to your destination. Many hotels also offer airport shuttle services for guests.

On the Rails: Public Transportation by Train

While Cyprus doesn't have a comprehensive railway network, the island's history is intertwined with charming vintage trains that once traversed its landscapes. Although these historic trains are no longer in operation for daily transportation, they contribute to the island's nostalgic charm.

1. **Cyprus Railway Museum:** To step back in time and explore the island's railway heritage, visit the Cyprus Railway Museum in Evrychou. The museum showcases vintage trains, locomotives, and artifacts, offering a glimpse into the bygone era of rail travel in Cyprus. It's a delightful experience for both history enthusiasts and families.

2. **Exploring by Bike:** For eco-conscious travelers and those seeking an active exploration, cycling is a popular and eco-friendly mode of transportation in Cyprus. Many towns and cities have designated bike lanes, and the island's diverse terrain offers cycling enthusiasts a range of trails, from coastal

paths to mountain routes.

3. **Renting a Bike:** Renting a bike is a convenient option for short-distance travel within urban areas or along scenic routes. Bike rental shops are available in major towns, and many coastal areas provide a pleasant backdrop for cycling adventures. Explore the island at your own pace, taking in the sights and sounds of Cyprus on two wheels.

The Pulse of Urban Life: Getting Around Towns

As you delve into the heart of Cypriot urban life, exploring towns and cities becomes a dynamic experience shaped by diverse modes of transportation.

1. **Walking Through History:** Many Cypriot towns and cities, especially in the older quarters, are best explored on foot. Stroll through narrow cobblestone streets, where historical sites, charming cafes, and local shops beckon. Walking not only allows you to absorb the rich history but also provides an intimate connection with the vibrant urban atmosphere.

2. **Public Buses:** Public buses are a reliable and cost-effective means of getting around towns and cities. In urban centers like Nicosia, Limassol, and Larnaca, buses connect key areas, making it convenient for both residents and visitors to navigate the urban landscape. Check local schedules and routes to plan your city exploration.

3. **Taxis and Ride-Sharing:** Taxis are readily available in urban areas, offering a convenient door-to-door service. In addition to traditional taxis, ride-sharing services may also be available, providing an alternative for those who prefer app-based transportation options.

4. **City Cycling:** Many Cypriot cities are embracing cycling as a sustainable mode of urban transportation. Bike-sharing programs are emerging in some urban areas, allowing

residents and visitors to rent bikes for short trips around the city. Explore urban landscapes on two wheels, enjoying the freedom of city cycling.

Embracing the Unseen: Tips for Transportation in Cyprus

As you embark on your transportation odyssey in Cyprus, consider these tips to enhance your travel experience:

1. **Plan Ahead:** Whether you're renting a car, taking a ferry, or flying to Cyprus, planning ahead ensures a smoother travel experience. Research transportation options, book tickets in advance, and familiarize yourself with schedules to optimize your time on the island.
2. **Weather Considerations:** Cyprus enjoys a Mediterranean climate, with hot summers and mild winters. Be mindful of weather conditions, especially if you plan to explore mountainous areas or coastal regions. Summer temperatures can be high, so stay hydrated and plan outdoor activities accordingly.
3. **Cultural Awareness:** Respect local customs and cultural norms when using transportation services. For example, in rural areas, buses may operate on a more relaxed schedule, so patience is key. In urban centers, be aware of peak traffic hours and plan accordingly.
4. **Language Essentials:** While English is widely spoken, especially in tourist areas, learning a few basic phrases in Greek or Turkish can enhance your interactions and add a personal touch to your travel experience. Locals appreciate the effort to connect in their native languages.
5. **Explore Off the Beaten Path:** Cyprus is not just about popular tourist destinations; the true essence of the island often lies off the beaten path. Consider exploring lesser-known villages, hidden beaches, and rural landscapes. Local

transportation options may provide a glimpse into the authentic Cypriot way of life.

6. **Safety First:** Prioritize safety when using different modes of transportation. Whether you're driving, cycling, or taking a ferry, adhere to safety guidelines and regulations. Be vigilant on the roads, especially in unfamiliar areas, and take necessary precautions for water-based activities.

7. **Connect with Locals:** Transportation experiences in Cyprus can become memorable encounters with locals. Strike up conversations with fellow travelers, ask for recommendations from locals, and embrace the opportunity to connect with the community. Local insights often lead to hidden gems and authentic experiences.

The Final Note: A Journey of Discoveries

As we conclude our exploration of transportation in Cyprus, envision your journey as a tapestry woven with the threads of road trips, maritime adventures, and the wings of air travel. Cyprus, with its diverse landscapes and rich cultural tapestry, invites you to embark on a journey of discoveries – both seen and unseen.

Whether you're navigating the roads with the sun on your face, setting sail on the Mediterranean waves, or soaring through the skies with the island beneath your wings, each mode of transportation becomes a chapter in your Cypriot story. As you traverse this enchanting island, may the pulse of transportation be the rhythmic heartbeat that connects you to the vibrant spirit of Cyprus – a place where every journey becomes a celebration of exploration, culture, and the timeless beauty of discovery. Safe travels on your Cypriot adventure!

Chapter 11
Leisure and Recreation

Welcome to the vibrant realm of leisure and recreation in Cyprus, where the sun-drenched landscapes beckon, and the island's rich tapestry of culture and nature unfolds before your eyes. As you embark on this chapter of your Cypriot journey, prepare to immerse yourself in a diverse array of activities that cater to every passion and inclination. Whether you seek the tranquility of pristine beaches, the thrill of outdoor adventures, or the cultural richness embedded in every corner, Cyprus offers a tapestry of leisure experiences that promises to elevate your sojourn to unforgettable heights.

Sun-Kissed Serenity: Cyprus Beaches

Let the allure of the Mediterranean draw you to the sun-kissed beaches that fringe the Cypriot coastline. Whether you crave the lively atmosphere of popular resorts or the secluded tranquility of hidden coves, Cyprus unveils a mosaic of beaches that cater to every preference.

1. **Ayia Napa Beaches:** Ayia Napa, renowned for its vibrant nightlife, is also home to some of the island's most famous beaches. Nissi Beach, with its golden sands and crystal-clear waters, is a hub for water sports and beach parties. Makronissos Beach, surrounded by nature trails, offers a serene escape for those seeking a quieter coastal retreat.

2. **Limassol Promenade:** Limassol, with its lively promenade, invites you to stroll along the sandy shores while enjoying breathtaking views of the Mediterranean. The city's beaches, including Lady's Mile and Dasoudi, are perfect for unwinding under the sun or indulging in water activities.

3. **Latchi and Akamas Peninsula:** For those desiring a more secluded coastal experience, the beaches around Latchi and

the Akamas Peninsula beckon. Explore the untouched beauty
of Lara Beach, known for its sea turtles, or indulge in the
pristine landscapes of the Blue Lagoon, accessible by boat.

4. **Coral Bay:** Nestled on the western coast of Cyprus, Coral
   Bay boasts a Blue Flag beach with golden sands and shallow
   waters. The beach is surrounded by restaurants and bars,
   making it an ideal spot for a day of relaxation and seaside
   indulgence.

Outdoor Escapades: Adventures in Nature

Cyprus, with its diverse topography, provides a playground for outdoor enthusiasts. Whether you're drawn to the rugged trails of the
Troodos Mountains or the coastal paths that offer panoramic views, the
island's natural wonders set the stage for exhilarating adventures.

1. **Troodos Trails:** Lace up your hiking boots and explore the
   network of trails that crisscross the Troodos Mountains.
   Mount Olympus, the island's highest peak, offers challenging
   hikes rewarded with panoramic vistas. Nature trails like the
   Artemis and Caledonia Falls trails invite you to discover the
   lush beauty of the mountainous landscapes.

2. **Cycling Adventures:** For cycling enthusiasts, Cyprus
   presents a network of cycling trails that cater to all skill levels.
   From the challenging climbs of the Troodos Mountains to
   scenic coastal routes, biking allows you to explore the island's
   diverse landscapes at your own pace.

3. **Akamas Adventures:** The Akamas Peninsula, a haven of
   biodiversity, invites nature lovers to embark on unforgettable
   adventures. Explore the Akamas Gorge, kayak along the
   rugged coastline, or embark on a 4x4 safari to uncover the
   untamed beauty of this pristine wilderness.

4. **Rock Climbing:** Thrill-seekers can test their mettle on the
   rock faces scattered across Cyprus. The limestone cliffs of

Kalymnos and the bouldering sites in the Troodos Mountains offer challenges for climbers of all levels. Whether you're a seasoned climber or a beginner, the island's rock formations promise an exhilarating experience.

Cultural Sojourns: Immersing in Heritage

As you traverse the historical landscapes of Cyprus, embark on cultural sojourns that unravel the island's rich heritage. From ancient ruins to medieval castles, each cultural gem invites you to step back in time and connect with the stories that shaped Cyprus.

1. **Ancient Kourion:** The archaeological site of Kourion, perched on a hill overlooking the sea, is a testament to Cyprus's ancient past. Explore the well-preserved amphitheater, the House of Eustolios, and the intricate mosaic floors that transport you to the Roman era.

2. **Medieval Magic in Limassol:** Limassol, with its medieval castle and historic old town, offers a journey through time. Wander through the narrow streets, where traditional Cypriot architecture blends with vibrant street art. The Limassol Castle, with its imposing presence, houses a medieval museum that delves into the island's history.

3. **Tombs of the Kings:** Paphos, a UNESCO World Heritage site, boasts the Tombs of the Kings – a necropolis dating back to the Hellenistic period. Marvel at the elaborate tombs carved into the rock and the intricate frescoes that adorn these ancient resting places.

4. **Nicosia's Cultural Tapestry:** The divided capital, Nicosia, invites you to explore its cultural tapestry. Wander through the narrow streets of the Old Town, where historic buildings coexist with modern cafes and boutiques. Visit the Cyprus Museum to delve into the island's archaeological treasures.

Gastronomic Delights: Culinary Explorations

No journey to Cyprus is complete without savoring the island's culinary treasures. From traditional meze feasts to seaside dining, Cyprus offers a gastronomic odyssey that tantalizes the taste buds and reflects the island's diverse cultural influences.

1. **Meze Marvels:** Indulge in the art of meze, a culinary tradition that transforms dining into a communal experience. Order a variety of small dishes, from halloumi and moussaka to souvlaki and fresh seafood. Meze is not just a meal; it's a celebration of flavors and shared moments.
2. **Seafood by the Shore:** With its extensive coastline, Cyprus is a haven for seafood enthusiasts. Coastal towns like Limassol and Larnaca boast seafood tavernas where you can relish the catch of the day with the sea breeze as your backdrop. Grilled octopus, calamari, and fresh fish are among the seaside delights awaiting your palate.
3. **Vineyard Ventures:** Cyprus, known for its wine-making traditions, invites you to explore its vineyard-dotted landscapes. Visit local wineries in regions like the Troodos foothills or the Paphos countryside to sample indigenous grape varieties. Commandaria, a sweet dessert wine with a rich history, is a must-try.
4. **Culinary Festivals:** If your visit aligns with one of Cyprus's culinary festivals, consider it a serendipitous delight. Festivals dedicated to wine, olives, and traditional Cypriot cuisine showcase the island's culinary heritage. Join locals in celebrating the harvest season or the richness of regional flavors.

Wellness Retreats: Nurturing Body and Soul

In the embrace of Cyprus's serene landscapes, wellness retreats offer a sanctuary for rejuvenation and self-discovery. From holistic spas to yoga retreats, the island's tranquil settings become the backdrop for nurturing your well-being.

1. **Spa Sanctuaries:** Cyprus is dotted with luxurious spa resorts that combine ancient wellness traditions with modern amenities. Surrender to the soothing touch of skilled therapists, indulge in rejuvenating treatments, and let the stresses of daily life melt away in the tranquil ambiance of spa sanctuaries.
2. **Yoga and Mindfulness:** Seek harmony of mind and body in Cyprus's yoga retreats. From beachfront sessions to mountain retreats, the island's diverse landscapes provide idyllic settings for yoga and mindfulness practices. Join a class, embrace the gentle flow of movement, and find your center amidst the natural beauty of Cyprus.
3. **Nature Meditation:** Connect with the healing power of nature through meditation in Cyprus's serene landscapes. Whether it's a secluded beach, a forested trail, or a mountain vantage point, the island's natural surroundings offer peaceful settings for mindfulness and meditation. Allow the sounds of nature to guide your inner journey.
4. **Hot Springs of Ayia Napa:** Ayia Napa, known for its lively atmosphere, also hides a secret haven of wellness – the Makronissos Tombs and hot springs. A dip in the warm waters of these natural springs is believed to have therapeutic benefits. Combine relaxation with a touch of ancient history as you immerse yourself in this unique wellness experience.

Connect with Locals: Community Experiences

As you delve into leisure and recreation in Cyprus, seize the opportunity to connect with the local community. Engage in activities that bring you closer to Cypriot traditions, foster connections, and leave you with lasting memories.

1. **Traditional Workshops:** Join traditional workshops where local artisans share their skills and crafts. Whether it's learning the art of Lefkaritika lace, pottery making, or basket weaving, these hands-on experiences provide insight into the island's cultural heritage. Create your own masterpiece to cherish as a memento of your Cypriot journey.

2. **Village Festivals:** Cyprus's villages come alive during traditional festivals, offering a glimpse into the heart of Cypriot life. Join locals in celebrating events like the Ayia Napa Medieval Festival or the Limassol Wine Festival. Engage in the festivities, savor local delicacies, and dance to the rhythms of traditional music.

3. **Farm-to-Table Experiences:** Delve into the agricultural traditions of Cyprus through farm-to-table experiences. Visit local farms, where you can pick fresh produce, participate in olive harvesting, or learn about traditional winemaking. These experiences not only connect you with the land but also provide an authentic taste of Cypriot rural life.

4. **Cultural Workshops:** Immerse yourself in the cultural fabric of Cyprus by attending cultural workshops. From traditional dance lessons to language exchange programs, these workshops offer opportunities to interact with locals, share stories, and foster cross-cultural connections.

The Culmination: Crafting Your Cypriot Tale

As we reach the culmination of our exploration into leisure and recreation in Cyprus, envision your journey as a tapestry woven with moments of seaside bliss, outdoor adventures, cultural immersions, and culinary delights. Cyprus, with its diverse offerings, invites you to craft your own Cypriot tale – a narrative shaped by the passions that ignite your spirit and the experiences that leave an indelible mark on your heart.

May your leisure pursuits in Cyprus be a symphony of discovery, a harmonious blend of relaxation and exploration that resonates with the rhythm of the island. Whether you find solace on a tranquil beach, exhilaration on a mountain trail, or inspiration in a cultural encounter, Cyprus unfolds as a canvas for your unique leisure and recreation odyssey.

As you continue your journey through this enchanting island, may each moment be a brushstroke that paints the canvas of your Cypriot tale. Whether you choose to bask in the Mediterranean sun, delve into the island's history, or savor the flavors of Cypriot cuisine, remember that every choice adds a vibrant hue to the masterpiece of your Cypriot adventure.

Craft your tale with intention, embrace the diversity of leisure experiences Cyprus offers, and let the island become not just a destination but a canvas for the creation of your own Cypriot masterpiece. As you explore, savor, and connect with the soul of Cyprus, may your leisure pursuits be the threads that weave a narrative of joy, discovery, and the timeless beauty of the Cypriot experience.

Chapter 12
Dealing with Challenges

Embarking on a journey to Cyprus is an exciting endeavor filled with the promise of discovery, adventure, and cultural enrichment. However, like any travel experience, it comes with its share of challenges. Navigating these challenges with resilience, adaptability, and a positive mindset is essential to ensuring a smooth and fulfilling journey. In this chapter, we'll delve into common challenges that travelers to Cyprus may encounter and offer practical insights on how to overcome them, turning obstacles into opportunities for growth and learning.

1. Language Barriers: The Art of Communication

One of the challenges travelers often face in a foreign land is the language barrier. While English is widely spoken in tourist areas and major cities in Cyprus, you may find that in more rural or off-the-beaten-path locations, locals predominantly converse in Greek or Turkish.

Navigating the Challenge:

- **Learn Basic Phrases:** Familiarize yourself with basic phrases in Greek or Turkish. Locals appreciate the effort, even if you only know a few words. Simple greetings, thank you, and polite expressions can go a long way in breaking down language barriers.
- **Translation Apps:** Make use of translation apps on your smartphone. These apps can assist in translating written or spoken words, helping you understand and communicate effectively. Offline versions can be particularly useful in areas with limited internet connectivity.
- **Local Language Classes:** Consider taking a short local language class or hiring a tutor for a few sessions before your

trip. Not only does this enhance your communication skills, but it also demonstrates your respect for the local culture.

2. Currency and Payment Issues: Navigating Finances

Handling currency and navigating payment methods in a new country can pose challenges. Cyprus uses the Euro (EUR), and while credit cards are widely accepted, some smaller establishments may prefer cash.

Navigating the Challenge:

- **Carry Cash:** Always carry some cash, especially when venturing into more remote areas. ATMs are readily available in major cities and towns, allowing you to withdraw cash in the local currency.
- **Inform Your Bank:** Notify your bank of your travel plans to avoid any issues with your credit or debit cards. Some banks may have security measures in place that could lead to card restrictions if they detect transactions from an unfamiliar location.
- **Currency Exchange:** Familiarize yourself with the current exchange rates, and consider exchanging a small amount of currency before your trip. While rates may be slightly better at local banks or exchange offices, having some cash on arrival can be convenient.

3. Transportation Hiccups: Navigating the Roads

Whether you're driving, taking public transportation, or using alternative modes like bicycles, unexpected transportation hiccups can occur. From road conditions to public transportation schedules, being prepared for disruptions can save you time and stress.

Navigating the Challenge:

- **Plan Your Routes:** Before embarking on road trips or using public transportation, plan your routes and check for any potential disruptions. Familiarize yourself with alternative routes and transportation options to mitigate unexpected delays.
- **Renting Vehicles:** If renting a car, inspect it thoroughly before accepting the keys. Take note of any pre-existing damage, and ensure that you understand the local traffic rules. In the event of a breakdown, contact the rental agency promptly for assistance.
- **Public Transportation Updates:** Stay informed about public transportation updates and schedules. Delays or changes in services can happen, so having up-to-date information allows you to adjust your plans accordingly.

4. Cultural Sensitivities: Embracing Differences

Cultural differences can be both enriching and challenging for travelers. Customs, traditions, and social norms in Cyprus may differ from what you're accustomed to, leading to moments of cultural sensitivity.

Navigating the Challenge:

- **Research Cultural Norms:** Before your trip, research and familiarize yourself with Cypriot cultural norms. Understanding local customs can help you navigate social situations with ease and respect.
- **Observe Locals:** Pay attention to how locals behave in various settings. Observing and emulating their behavior can help you integrate more seamlessly into the cultural fabric of Cyprus.
- **Ask for Guidance:** If you're unsure about a specific cultural practice, don't hesitate to ask for guidance. Locals are often happy to share insights and appreciate the effort you make to

respect their traditions.

5. Weather Surprises: Adapting to Climate Changes

Cyprus enjoys a Mediterranean climate, but weather conditions can vary, especially if you're traveling between different regions or during different seasons. Unexpected rain, strong winds, or intense heat may require adjustments to your plans.

Navigating the Challenge:

- **Check Weather Forecasts:** Stay updated on weather forecasts for the specific regions you plan to visit. This helps you pack appropriately and make adjustments to your itinerary based on predicted weather conditions.
- **Pack Layers:** Cyprus can experience temperature fluctuations, even within a single day. Packing layers allows you to adapt to changing weather conditions, whether you're exploring the cool Troodos Mountains or basking in the warmth of coastal areas.
- **Flexible Itinerary:** Have a flexible itinerary that allows for changes based on weather conditions. If outdoor activities are affected by weather, have alternative indoor options in mind.

6. Health and Medical Concerns: Prioritizing Well-being

Dealing with health-related challenges is a crucial aspect of travel. While Cyprus has a well-developed healthcare system, unexpected illnesses or accidents can happen.

Navigating the Challenge:

- **Travel Insurance:** Ensure you have comprehensive travel insurance that covers medical emergencies, including hospital stays and evacuation if necessary. Familiarize yourself with the terms and conditions of your insurance policy.

- **Carry Medications:** If you have specific medications, carry an ample supply for the duration of your trip. Familiarize yourself with the generic names of your medications, as brand names may vary.
- **Locate Medical Facilities:** Identify the locations of medical facilities, pharmacies, and emergency services in the areas you plan to visit. Having this information readily available can be invaluable in case of any health-related concerns.

7. Connectivity Challenges: Staying Connected

Staying connected is vital for various reasons, from navigation to communication. However, connectivity challenges such as limited internet access or unreliable mobile networks may arise.

Navigating the Challenge:

- **Offline Maps:** Download offline maps of the areas you plan to explore. This ensures you can navigate even in areas with poor internet connectivity.
- **Local SIM Card:** Consider purchasing a local SIM card upon arrival for reliable and cost-effective local data and call services. Check with your accommodation or local shops for options.
- **Wi-Fi Hotspots:** Identify Wi-Fi hotspots in your accommodation, restaurants, and public spaces. This allows you to stay connected when needed and save on mobile data usage.

8. Accommodation Issues: Resolving Lodging Concerns

While Cyprus offers a wide range of accommodation options, unexpected issues such as reservation problems or dissatisfaction with your lodging may arise.

Navigating the Challenge:

- **Check Reviews:** Before booking accommodation, read reviews from other travelers to gain insights into the quality and service of the property. This can help you make informed decisions.
- **Contact Accommodations Directly:** If you have specific requests or concerns, consider reaching out to the accommodation directly. This allows you to address any potential issues in advance and ensures clarity on your expectations.
- **Have Alternatives:** Always have a backup plan. In case of any unforeseen issues with your accommodation, knowing nearby alternatives can save you from last-minute stress.

9. Safety Concerns: Prioritizing Personal Safety

Maintaining personal safety is paramount in any travel destination. While Cyprus is generally considered safe, it's essential to be vigilant and aware of your surroundings.

Navigating the Challenge:

- **Stay Informed:** Stay informed about local safety guidelines and advisories. Check with your accommodation or local authorities for any specific precautions or areas to avoid.
- **Use Reputable Services:** Whether it's transportation, tours, or activities, opt for reputable and licensed services. This ensures a higher level of safety and reliability.
- **Emergency Contacts:** Save local emergency numbers in your phone, and inform someone you trust about your whereabouts. In case of any issues, having quick access to assistance is crucial.

10. Time Management: Embracing the Cypriot Pace

Cypriot culture often operates at a more relaxed pace compared to some Western societies. This might result in different expectations regarding service speed, transportation punctuality, or response times.

Navigating the Challenge:

- **Practice Patience:** Embrace the Cypriot concept of "siga siga" (slowly, slowly). Understand that the pace of life may be more leisurely, especially in rural areas. Practice patience and allow yourself to adapt to the local rhythm.
- **Plan Accordingly:** Factor in additional time for activities, transportation, or services. Avoid tight schedules that may lead to stress if things don't go exactly as planned.
- **Enjoy the Moment:** Use the opportunity to appreciate the present moment. Whether it's waiting for a meal or enjoying a leisurely stroll, the Cypriot pace encourages you to savor each experience.

Conclusion: Transforming Challenges into Triumphs

As you navigate the challenges that may arise during your journey in Cyprus, remember that each obstacle presents an opportunity for growth, learning, and a deeper connection with the destination. By approaching challenges with a positive mindset, adaptability, and a willingness to embrace the unknown, you not only overcome hurdles but also create enduring memories.

Travel is a transformative experience, and the challenges encountered along the way contribute to the richness of your journey. In Cyprus, as in any destination, the ability to navigate uncertainties with grace and resilience adds an extra layer of fulfillment to your adventure. Embrace the unexpected, learn from the challenges, and let every twist and turn in your Cypriot tale become a triumph in its own right. May your journey be not only about the destinations you reach but also about the person you become along the way. Safe travels!

Chapter 13
Celebrations and Festivals

Welcome to the lively tapestry of celebrations and festivals that color the calendar of Cyprus. As you traverse this enchanting island, you'll discover that Cypriots have mastered the art of combining tradition, joy, and a generous sprinkle of Mediterranean zest in their vibrant festivities. From religious celebrations that echo centuries-old customs to modern festivals that embrace the island's dynamic spirit, Cyprus invites you to join in the revelry and immerse yourself in the cultural heartbeat of the land.

A Symphony of Tradition: Religious Celebrations

Cyprus, with its rich religious heritage, hosts a plethora of celebrations that offer a glimpse into the island's devotion and time-honored customs. Whether you're a participant or an observer, these religious festivals provide a unique opportunity to witness the intersection of faith, community, and tradition.

Easter – A Resplendent Celebration: Easter holds a special place in the hearts of Cypriots, marking the most significant religious celebration of the year. The entire island comes alive with a sense of anticipation and devotion during Holy Week. From Palm Sunday processions to the somber Good Friday services, each day leads to the grand culmination of Easter Sunday.

Picture yourself in a village square adorned with flickering candles as the Resurrection Mass commences. The joyous "Christos Anesti" (Christ has risen) echoes through the night, followed by a jubilant feast. Join locals in savoring the traditional flaounes, a savory pastry filled with cheese and raisins, and experience the warmth of Cypriot hospitality during this momentous celebration.

Feast of Kataklysmos – A Watery Affair: Kataklysmos, also known as the Feast of the Flood, is a unique celebration that combines religious observance with lively festivities. Taking place 50 days after Easter, this event commemorates the biblical Flood and the salvation of Noah.

Head to coastal towns like Limassol, Larnaca, or Paphos during Kataklysmos, and you'll find a joyful atmosphere along the waterfront. Traditionally, people engage in water-related activities, symbolizing purification and renewal. Expect water games, boat races, and a vibrant market atmosphere. Join the locals in dancing to traditional music, indulging in festive treats, and celebrating the unity of faith and community.

Cultural Extravaganza: Limassol Wine Festival

Prepare your taste buds for an extraordinary journey through Cyprus's wine heritage at the Limassol Wine Festival. Held annually at the Municipal Gardens in Limassol, this festival transforms the city into a celebration of Dionysian proportions. As you enter the festival grounds, you'll be greeted by the aroma of local wines and the sounds of traditional music.

Sample an array of Cypriot wines, from robust reds to crisp whites, as local winemakers showcase their craftsmanship. Engage in the age-old tradition of stomping grapes and immerse yourself in the vibrant atmosphere of dance and music performances. The Limassol Wine Festival is not just an event for wine enthusiasts; it's a cultural extravaganza that celebrates the island's winemaking heritage with zest and revelry.

Medieval Marvels: Ayia Napa Medieval Festival

Transport yourself back in time to the days of knights, princesses, and medieval merriment at the Ayia Napa Medieval Festival. Held in the historic Monastery of Ayia Napa, this festival is a captivating blend of history, entertainment, and vibrant pageantry.

As you wander through the cobbled streets, you'll encounter jugglers, minstrels, and knights in shining armor. Revel in live performances that bring medieval tales to life, and indulge in a feast fit for royalty. The Ayia Napa Medieval Festival is a testament to the island's ability to seamlessly blend its rich history with modern celebrations, creating an event that captivates both locals and visitors alike.

Harvest Celebrations: Wine and Gastronomy Festivals

Cyprus, with its fertile landscapes and centuries-old agricultural traditions, pays homage to the bounties of the land through various wine and gastronomy festivals. These celebrations are a sensory journey, inviting you to savor the flavors of the island, from freshly harvested fruits to exquisite wines.

Wine Festival of Cyprus: The Wine Festival of Cyprus is a celebration of the island's winemaking prowess, taking place annually in the enchanting setting of the Limassol Municipal Gardens. Here, you'll discover an extensive array of local wines, from the renowned Commandaria to the distinct Maratheftiko and Xynisteri varieties.

Participate in wine-tasting sessions led by knowledgeable sommeliers, and learn about the intricate art of winemaking. Accompany your tastings with traditional Cypriot delicacies, and engage in the festive spirit as music and dance performances fill the air. The Wine Festival of Cyprus is a culinary journey that unveils the island's viticultural treasures.

Almond Blossom Festival: As winter bids farewell, Cyprus dresses in a delicate coat of almond blossoms, signaling the arrival of spring. The Almond Blossom Festival, celebrated in various villages such as Limnatis and Agros, honors this natural spectacle and the abundance of almonds.

Picture yourself strolling through orchards adorned with blossoms, accompanied by the sweet fragrance of almonds in the air. Indulge in almond-based delicacies, from marzipan sweets to almond-infused pastries. The festival is not just a culinary delight but a visual feast that captures the essence of renewal and the awakening of nature.

Modern Rhythms: Music and Cultural Festivals

Beyond traditional celebrations, Cyprus embraces modern rhythms through music and cultural festivals that cater to diverse tastes.

From international artists gracing the stage to local talents showcasing their prowess, these festivals add a contemporary flair to the island's cultural landscape.

Ayia Napa International Festival: Ayia Napa, known for its vibrant nightlife, transforms into a cultural haven during the Ayia Napa International Festival. This event attracts a diverse array of performers, from musicians and dancers to artists and street performers. The festival is a celebration of artistic expression, with live shows, exhibitions, and interactive performances that captivate audiences of all ages.

Immerse yourself in the kaleidoscope of creativity as the streets come alive with color, music, and theatrical displays. The Ayia Napa International Festival is a testament to the island's ability to fuse its historical charm with contemporary cultural expressions, creating an event that resonates with the modern spirit of Cyprus.

Navigating Festivals: Tips for a Joyous Experience

As you prepare to partake in the celebratory tapestry of Cyprus, consider these tips to enhance your festival experience:

1. **Check Festival Dates:** Research the dates of specific festivals before your trip, and plan your itinerary accordingly. Festivals are often linked to religious or seasonal events, so understanding their timing adds depth to your cultural immersion.

2. **Respect Local Customs:** During religious festivals, respect local customs and practices. Be mindful of appropriate attire and observe any traditions that accompany the celebrations. Engaging with locals in a respectful manner enhances the authenticity of your experience.

3. **Embrace the Festive Spirit:** Allow yourself to fully embrace the festive spirit by participating in activities, trying traditional foods, and joining in the dances. Festivals are a communal celebration, and your willingness to engage adds

to the joyous atmosphere.

4. **Capture Moments:** Festivals in Cyprus are a visual and sensory feast. Capture moments through photographs, but also take time to put the camera aside and fully immerse yourself in the experience. Let the sights, sounds, and aromas become lasting memories.

5. **Plan Ahead:** For popular festivals, especially those with international acclaim, plan ahead and consider booking accommodations in advance. Festivals can draw large crowds, and securing your stay ensures a more relaxed and enjoyable experience.

Conclusion: A Tapestry of Celebration

As you step into the realm of celebrations and festivals in Cyprus, you embark on a journey that transcends time and tradition. The island's vibrant tapestry is woven with threads of faith, culture, and the indomitable spirit of celebration. Whether you find yourself dancing under the stars during Kataklysmos or toasting to the richness of Commandaria at the Wine Festival, each festival in Cyprus invites you to become part of its narrative.

As you navigate the cultural nuances, savor the culinary delights, and embrace the harmonies of traditional and modern music, remember that these festivals are not just events; they are windows into the soul of Cyprus. The island's celebrations are an invitation to join hands with locals, share in their joy, and become a part of the living legacy that defines the Cypriot spirit.

So, let the music guide your steps, let the flavors tantalize your taste buds, and let the laughter of the locals become the soundtrack of your festival journey. May each celebration be a brushstroke on the canvas of your Cypriot adventure, adding depth, color, and an enduring sense of connection to the heart of this captivating island. As you join in the revelry and immerse yourself in the festive spirit, may you find not just celebrations but moments of shared joy that resonate with the timeless melody of Cyprus. Cheers to the tapestry of celebration that awaits you on this enchanting island!

Chapter 14
Safety and Security

In the grand tapestry of travel, woven with threads of adventure and discovery, the importance of safety and security stands as a foundational pillar. As you embark on your journey to Cyprus, a land where ancient history meets modern charm, ensuring your well-being becomes paramount. This chapter serves as a guide, offering insights, practical tips, and a reassuring voice to help you navigate the nuances of safety, making your Cypriot adventure not only memorable but also secure.

A Mosaic of Safety: Cyprus Overview

Cyprus, known for its warm hospitality and inviting landscapes, is generally considered a safe destination for travelers. The island's low crime rates contribute to an environment where visitors can explore with a sense of ease. However, as with any travel destination, it's essential to remain vigilant and informed to ensure a smooth and secure experience.

Cypriot Hospitality: One of the hallmarks of Cyprus is the genuine warmth and hospitality of its people. Locals are often welcoming and ready to assist travelers, contributing to a sense of safety and camaraderie. Whether you're strolling through vibrant marketplaces or seeking directions, don't hesitate to engage with the friendly Cypriot community.

Healthcare Standards: Cyprus boasts a well-developed healthcare system, with modern medical facilities and proficient medical professionals. European Union citizens can access emergency medical treatment with the European Health Insurance Card (EHIC). For non-EU citizens, comprehensive travel insurance that covers medical expenses is strongly recommended.

Political Situation: The political situation in Cyprus has seen periods of tension, particularly in relation to the division of the island.

The Republic of Cyprus, a member of the European Union, governs the southern part of the island, while the northern part is administered by the Turkish Republic of Northern Cyprus. Travelers are advised to stay informed about the geopolitical landscape and adhere to any travel advisories issued by their respective governments.

Navigating Public Spaces: Urban and Rural Safety

Whether you find yourself in the bustling streets of Nicosia or the tranquil villages of Troodos, understanding the dynamics of urban and rural safety enhances your overall travel experience.

Urban Vigilance: In urban areas, exercise the same vigilance you would in any city. Be mindful of your belongings, particularly in crowded places and public transportation. Keep a close eye on your wallet, secure your bags, and avoid displaying valuable items openly. While instances of petty crime are relatively low, preventive measures go a long way.

Transportation Safety: Cyprus offers a variety of transportation options, from well-maintained roads for self-driving to public buses and taxis. If you're renting a car, adhere to traffic rules, and familiarize yourself with local driving habits. Public transportation is generally safe, but be cautious with your belongings, especially during peak travel times.

Rural Tranquility: Exploring the rural landscapes of Cyprus is a delightful experience, offering a glimpse into traditional Cypriot life. In villages and remote areas, the pace is slower, and the sense of community is strong. While crime rates are minimal, it's advisable to respect local customs and privacy. If you plan to hike or engage in outdoor activities, inform someone about your plans and carry essentials like water, a map, and a charged phone.

Accommodation Awareness: Choosing Safe Stays

Selecting accommodation is a crucial aspect of your journey, and ensuring your safety begins with choosing reputable and secure lodgings.

Research and Reviews: Before booking accommodation, conduct thorough research and read reviews from fellow travelers. Platforms like online booking websites and travel forums provide valuable insights into the safety, cleanliness, and service quality of various establishments. Look for accommodations with positive reviews regarding security measures and guest experiences.

Communication with Hosts: If you have specific safety concerns or requirements, don't hesitate to communicate with the accommodation directly. Reputable hosts prioritize the well-being of their guests and are often willing to address any questions or concerns you may have. Confirming details about security features and emergency procedures contributes to a sense of assurance.

Emergency Information: Upon arrival, familiarize yourself with emergency information provided by your accommodation. Know the location of fire exits, emergency contact numbers, and any specific safety protocols in place. Being informed about these aspects ensures you can respond calmly in case of any unforeseen situations.

Navigating Natural Elements: Weather and Outdoor Safety

Cyprus, with its diverse landscapes, invites exploration of natural wonders, from the sun-drenched beaches to the mountainous terrains. Understanding and respecting the elements is essential for a safe and enjoyable outdoor experience.

Weather Awareness: The Mediterranean climate of Cyprus means warm, dry summers and mild winters. However, weather conditions can vary, especially between coastal and mountainous regions. Check weather forecasts before embarking on outdoor activities, and pack accordingly. Carry essentials such as sunscreen, hats, and sufficient water to stay hydrated, particularly during hot summer days.

Mountain Safety: If you plan to explore the Troodos Mountains, where lush forests and picturesque trails await, prioritize mountain safety. Inform someone about your hiking plans, choose marked trails, and stay on designated paths. Weather conditions in the mountains can change rapidly, so be prepared for temperature variations and the possibility of rain.

Beach Caution: Cyprus boasts stunning beaches with crystal-clear waters, perfect for relaxation and water activities. While enjoying the coast, be cautious of strong currents, especially during the winter months. Heed warning signs, and if you're not a strong swimmer, stick to designated swimming areas. Sunbeds and umbrellas are often available for rent, providing a comfortable and safer beach experience.

Culinary Explorations: Food Safety and Hygiene

Sampling the rich tapestry of Cypriot cuisine is a delightful journey for your taste buds, and ensuring food safety enhances this gastronomic adventure.

Hygiene Standards: Cypriot restaurants and eateries generally adhere to high hygiene standards. When dining out, opt for establishments with a clean and well-maintained appearance. While street food is a popular option, ensure that vendors follow proper food handling practices.

Water Safety: Tap water in Cyprus is considered safe for consumption, but if you have any concerns, bottled water is widely available. When exploring outdoor areas or engaging in physical activities, staying hydrated is crucial. Carry a reusable water bottle to reduce environmental impact and ensure a continuous supply of water.

Food Allergies and Preferences: If you have food allergies or specific dietary preferences, communicate these clearly when dining out. Cypriot cuisine is diverse, with options for vegetarians, vegans, and individuals with various dietary requirements. Engaging with local chefs and staff about your preferences ensures a pleasant and safe dining experience.

Cultural Respect: Navigating Social Interactions

Respecting local customs and cultural nuances is fundamental to a harmonious and secure travel experience in Cyprus.

Attire Consideration: Cypriots, while generally open-minded, appreciate modesty in attire, especially in religious or rural areas. When visiting churches or monasteries, it's advisable to dress modestly, covering shoulders and knees. Adhering to dress codes not only shows cultural respect but also ensures a seamless exploration of historical and religious sites.

Photography Etiquette: Capturing the beauty of Cyprus through photographs is a cherished part of your journey. However, exercise discretion, particularly in areas where photography may be restricted, such as military installations or private properties. Respect the privacy of locals, and ask for permission before taking photos of individuals.

Greetings and Gestures: Engage with locals with a friendly demeanor, and embrace common greetings such as "Kalimera" (Good morning) and "Kalispera" (Good evening). Handshakes are a common form of greeting, and a polite nod is considered respectful. Understanding and practicing these simple gestures contribute to positive social interactions.

Technology and Connectivity: Staying Connected Safely

In an age where technology plays a crucial role in travel, ensuring the safety of your digital presence is equally important.

Secure Internet Connections: When using public Wi-Fi, exercise caution, and avoid accessing sensitive information such as online banking or private emails. Consider using Virtual Private Network (VPN) services to enhance the security of your internet connection, particularly when accessing public networks in cafes, hotels, or airports.

Protecting Personal Devices: Keep your personal devices secure by using strong passwords and enabling features such as biometric authentication. Install reliable antivirus software on your devices before your journey. In case of theft or loss, having remote tracking and data-wiping capabilities can safeguard your sensitive information.

Emergency Apps and Contacts: Download local emergency apps or store relevant emergency contacts in your phone. Being prepared for unforeseen situations, whether medical emergencies or other concerns, ensures you can access assistance swiftly.

Personal Safety Measures: Empowering Your Journey

While Cyprus offers a generally safe environment, adopting personal safety measures empowers you to navigate your journey with confidence.

Travel Insurance: Comprehensive travel insurance is a non-negotiable aspect of travel preparedness. Ensure your insurance covers medical emergencies, trip cancellations, and potential travel disruptions. Familiarize yourself with the terms and conditions of your insurance policy to guarantee a seamless claims process if needed.

Emergency Contact Information: Carry a list of emergency contact numbers, including local authorities, your country's embassy or consulate, and your accommodation's emergency contact. Having this information readily available can prove invaluable in critical situations.

Solo Travel Precautions: If you're traveling solo, inform someone you trust about your itinerary and check in regularly. Share your location with a trusted contact using mobile apps or messaging features. Stay in well-populated areas, especially during nighttime, and trust your instincts.

Conclusion: Your Safety, Your Journey

As you navigate the myriad wonders of Cyprus, remember that your safety is not just a consideration but a priority. By blending cultural respect with technological awareness and personal preparedness, you create a secure framework for your exploration.

Cyprus, with its mosaic of landscapes, rich history, and inviting culture, awaits your discovery. Let each step be a testament to your ability to explore with both curiosity and caution, to embrace adventure while safeguarding your well-being. May your journey through this captivating island be not only memorable but also a testament to the harmonious blend of safety and exploration.

As you embark on your Cypriot adventure, may the warmth of the Mediterranean sun be accompanied by the assurance of a secure and enriching journey. Safe travels, and may the experiences that unfold become cherished chapters in the story of your Cyprus exploration!

Chapter 15
Sustaining a Fulfilling Life

In the symphony of life, each journey we undertake is a melody composed of experiences, connections, and the pursuit of fulfillment. As you find yourself immersed in the enchanting landscapes of Cyprus, it's not just about the places you visit but the life you cultivate during your stay. This chapter is a guide to sustaining a fulfilling life on this captivating island—a roadmap to infusing your days with meaning, embracing the Cypriot lifestyle, and creating a mosaic of memories that endure long after your journey concludes.

The Art of Slow Living: Embracing Cypriot Time

In the heart of Cyprus beats a rhythm known as "siga siga"—slowly, slowly. The Cypriot concept of time is a departure from the hurried pace of modern life. It's an invitation to savor each moment, relish the simplicity of daily experiences, and embrace the beauty of unhurried living.

Morning Rituals: Begin your day with the unhurried pace that characterizes Cypriot mornings. Picture yourself in a village square, sipping a cup of freshly brewed coffee at a local café. Engage in friendly conversations with locals, allowing the morning sun to cast a golden glow on the cobblestone streets. Embracing the morning rituals becomes a cornerstone of the fulfilling life you seek.

Afternoon Siestas: In the warmth of the afternoon, when the sun reaches its zenith, Cyprus takes a collective pause for siesta. Follow suit by retreating to the shade, indulging in a leisurely lunch, or finding a tranquil spot to rest. The siesta is not just a nap; it's a cultural practice that rejuvenates both body and spirit, paving the way for a more energized and fulfilling afternoon.

Evening Strolls: As the sun begins its descent, embark on leisurely evening strolls. Whether along the coast, through charming villages, or in the midst of bustling towns, the evening is a canvas for serenity and connection. Engage in the Cypriot tradition of the "volta," a slow-paced walk where conversation flows, laughter resonates, and the simple act of being together takes precedence.

Nourishing the Body and Soul: Cypriot Cuisine and Lifestyle

The essence of a fulfilling life in Cyprus is intertwined with the island's rich culinary heritage and the celebration of nourishment, not just for the body but for the soul.

Mediterranean Diet: Indulge in the bounty of the Mediterranean diet, a cornerstone of Cypriot gastronomy. Fresh fruits, vegetables, olive oil, grains, and lean proteins form the basis of meals, contributing not only to physical well-being but also to a sense of vitality. Allow your taste buds to dance with the flavors of halloumi cheese, souvlaki, and the renowned Cypriot meze—an array of small dishes that transform dining into a shared celebration.

Farm-to-Table Connections: Explore local markets and embrace the farm-to-table lifestyle that defines Cypriot culinary traditions. Engage with farmers and artisans, learning about the origins of your food. The act of selecting fresh produce, artisanal cheeses, and locally sourced goods becomes a ritual that connects you to the land and the people who cultivate its abundance.

Wine and Communion: Wine, deeply embedded in Cypriot culture, is not just a beverage but a conduit for connection and communion. Attend wine festivals, visit vineyards, and savor the complexity of Cypriot wines. Whether enjoying a glass with a meal or partaking in a toast during celebrations, wine becomes a companion on your journey, intertwining moments of joy with the terroir of Cyprus.

Nature's Bounty: Outdoor Exploration and Well-being

As you navigate the diverse landscapes of Cyprus, from golden beaches to verdant mountains, the outdoors becomes a canvas for well-being and a conduit for a fulfilling life.

Hiking Tranquility: Discover the therapeutic benefits of hiking in the Troodos Mountains. Immerse yourself in the tranquility of pine-scented forests, where the rustling leaves and bird songs become a symphony of nature. Hiking not only nurtures physical health but also offers moments of introspection and connection with the natural world.

Sea and Serenity: Allow the rhythmic lull of the Mediterranean Sea to be a source of serenity. Whether lounging on pristine beaches, engaging in water activities, or simply gazing at the horizon, the sea becomes a therapeutic backdrop for relaxation. Let the sound of waves and the touch of sea breeze rejuvenate your senses, contributing to a life well-lived.

Stargazing Reflections: In the tranquil evenings of Cyprus, away from the urban glow, the night sky unveils a celestial spectacle. Engage in the timeless practice of stargazing, where the constellations become storytellers of the cosmos. The act of looking up, contemplating the vastness of the universe, becomes a meditative journey that transcends the ordinary and invites reflection.

Cultural Immersion: Connecting with Community

A fulfilling life in Cyprus extends beyond personal experiences to the connections forged with the vibrant community that calls the island home.

Local Festivals: Participate in local celebrations and festivals that punctuate the Cypriot calendar. Whether it's the joyous Easter festivities, the lively Kataklysmos, or the cultural extravaganzas of music and arts, these events offer a window into the heart of Cypriot life. Engage with locals, share in their traditions, and become part of the collective tapestry of celebration.

Community Engagement: Contribute to the community by engaging in local initiatives and volunteering opportunities. Whether it's participating in environmental conservation projects, supporting local artisans, or getting involved in educational programs, your active participation fosters a sense of belonging and purpose. As you share your skills and time, you become an integral part of the community's story.

Language Integration: Language is a bridge that connects cultures, and learning a few phrases in Greek enhances your cultural integration. Embrace the beauty of the Greek language, whether it's exchanging pleasantries with locals, navigating markets, or immersing yourself in conversations. The effort to speak the language is not just a practical skill but a gesture of respect that deepens your connection with the community.

Artistic Expression: Unleashing Creativity

In the pursuit of a fulfilling life, Cyprus becomes a canvas for artistic expression, inviting you to unleash your creativity and embrace the transformative power of the arts.

Inspired by Heritage: Draw inspiration from the rich heritage of Cyprus to embark on creative endeavors. Whether it's capturing the essence of ancient ruins through photography, expressing the vibrant colors of the landscape through painting, or translating the rhythms of the island into music, artistic pursuits become a conduit for self-discovery and connection.

Craftsmanship and Artisanal Traditions: Immerse yourself in the artisanal traditions of Cyprus, from pottery and weaving to intricate lacework. Engage in workshops with local craftsmen, learning the techniques passed down through generations. The act of creating with your hands becomes a meditative practice, grounding you in the present and fostering a sense of accomplishment.

Literary Explorations: As you wander through the historic streets of Cyprus, let the landscape inspire your literary explorations. Whether it's journaling about your experiences, penning poems inspired by the sea, or delving into the works of Cypriot authors, words become a medium for introspection and storytelling. The literary tapestry you weave becomes a personal narrative of your journey.

Balancing Reflection and Exploration: Mindful Living

In the pursuit of a fulfilling life, the balance between reflection and exploration becomes a dynamic dance—a harmonious interplay that enriches each moment.

Mindfulness Practices: Integrate mindfulness practices into your daily routine, whether through meditation, yoga, or mindful walks. Embrace the present moment, allowing the sights, sounds, and sensations of Cyprus to unfold with heightened awareness. Mindfulness becomes a compass that guides you through the labyrinth of experiences, fostering a deeper connection with yourself and the world around you.

Reflective Journeys: Carve out moments for reflection amid the tapestry of exploration. Journaling about your experiences, aspirations, and insights becomes a reflective journey that adds depth to your narrative. Whether under the shade of a centuries-old tree or overlooking the azure sea, these moments of contemplation become stepping stones toward a more conscious and fulfilling life.

Exploration of Inner Landscapes: As you traverse the external landscapes of Cyprus, embark on an exploration of your inner landscapes. Engage in activities that nourish your soul—whether it's reading a book by the beach, practicing a creative craft, or simply relishing the silence of a quiet village. The integration of inner exploration with external discovery becomes a holistic approach to a life well-lived.

Connection to Legacy: Leaving a Lasting Impact

A fulfilling life in Cyprus extends beyond personal gratification; it encompasses the legacy you leave behind and the impact you have on the communities and environments you encounter.

Sustainable Practices: Adopt sustainable practices that align with the ethos of Cyprus's natural beauty. Reduce single-use plastic, support eco-friendly initiatives, and make choices that minimize your ecological footprint. Engage in responsible tourism practices that contribute to the preservation of the island's pristine landscapes for generations to come.

Educational Exchange: If your journey involves an extended stay, consider engaging in educational exchange. Share your knowledge and skills with local communities, whether through language classes, workshops, or collaborative projects. In turn, embrace the opportunity to learn from the wisdom and traditions of the Cypriot people. This reciprocal exchange becomes a testament to the transformative power of cultural connection.

Legacy of Connection: As you bid farewell to Cyprus, leave behind a legacy of connection and goodwill. Stay in touch with the friends you've made, whether through letters, emails, or virtual connections. The relationships forged become threads in the fabric of your Cypriot journey, enduring beyond geographical boundaries.

Conclusion: A Life Well-Lived in Cyprus

As you navigate the landscape of a fulfilling life in Cyprus, remember that the essence of your journey lies not just in the places you visit but in the life you cultivate along the way. Cyprus, with its ancient history, warm hospitality, and diverse landscapes, becomes a canvas for your unique tapestry of experiences.

May each day be a celebration of siya siga, an embrace of slow living that allows you to savor the richness of each moment. May your culinary explorations be a symphony of flavors that dance on your palate and linger in your memories. May the outdoor landscapes become a sanctuary for well-being, a canvas for artistic expression, and a classroom for cultural immersion.

As you balance reflection with exploration, may your journey be a mindful dance—a harmonious interplay that enriches your soul. And as you connect with the community, leaving behind a legacy of goodwill, may your life in Cyprus be a testament to the transformative power of travel.

In the grand tapestry of your Cypriot adventure, may you find not just moments but a mosaic of fulfillment—a life well-lived on this enchanting island. As you carry the memories, lessons, and connections with you, may Cyprus forever hold a special place in the story of your life's journey. Cheers to sustaining a fulfilling life in the embrace of Cyprus!

Epilogue
A Tapestry Unfurls

As the final chapter unfolds, we find ourselves at the crossroads of re-flection and anticipation, poised on the threshold of what lies ahead. Your journey to Cyprus, from the first inklings of curiosity to the foot-steps echoing through ancient landscapes, has been a tapestry woven with the threads of discovery, connection, and transformation. The epi-logue is not just a conclusion but an invitation to contemplate the essence of your Cypriot adventure—a tale that transcends the bound-aries of time and geography.

Reflecting on the Journey

Pause for a moment and reflect on the odyssey that brought you to Cyprus. The vibrant markets, the echoes of ancient civilizations, the azure waters caressing golden shores—each chapter a stroke on the can-vas of your travel memoir. Consider the faces you've encountered, the flavors that linger on your palate, and the landscapes etched in your memory. In these reflections, you uncover not just the places you visit-ed but the profound impact they've left on your soul.

The Unseen Chapters: Every journey conceals unseen chapters, mo-ments that transcend guidebooks and itineraries. It's the laughter shared with locals over a cup of coffee, the serendipitous encounters in hidden alleys, and the quiet contemplation amid nature's embrace. As you reflect on these intangible moments, you realize they form the soulful core of your Cypriot experience—a mosaic of the unexpected, the unscripted, and the extraordinary.

Personal Growth and Transformation: Travel is a catalyst for per-sonal growth, a journey that extends beyond geographical boundaries into the realm of self-discovery. Consider the ways in which Cyprus has been a catalyst for transformation. Whether it's gaining a deeper appre-ciation for cultural nuances, embracing the art of slow living, or discovering hidden facets of your own resilience, your journey has been a tapestry of evolution.

Lessons from the Island of Aphrodite

Cyprus, the mythical birthplace of Aphrodite, the goddess of love and beauty, imparts lessons that extend beyond its sun-kissed shores. These lessons are the echoes of ancient wisdom, the whispers of sea breezes, and the resonance of history written in stone.

The Art of Connection: In the embrace of Cyprus, you've learned the art of connection—the ability to transcend language barriers and cultural differences through shared moments and genuine gestures. The island's inhabitants, with their warmth and hospitality, have been more than guides; they've been architects of connection, weaving you into the fabric of Cypriot life.

Savoring Time: The Cypriot concept of "siga siga," or slowly slowly, has permeated your journey, inviting you to savor time rather than merely pass through it. In a world that often races forward, Cyprus teaches the value of unhurried living, where moments are not counted but cherished, and each experience is a layer added to the richness of life.

Cultural Resilience: The island's history, marked by invasions, struggles, and triumphs, reveals a resilience that extends beyond the physical landscapes. Cyprus stands as a testament to the enduring spirit of its people—a resilience that transforms challenges into opportunities and adversity into strength. In embracing this resilience, you've not only witnessed history but become a part of the island's living narrative.

Carrying Cyprus with You

As you stand at the conclusion of this chapter, the question arises: How will you carry Cyprus with you as you journey forward? The island's imprint is not confined to photographs and souvenirs; it resides in the intangible aspects of your being.

The Essence of Slow Living: Bring the art of slow living into your daily existence. Whether it's savoring a cup of coffee with mindful awareness or infusing your routine with moments of deliberate slowness, let the Cypriot concept of time become a guiding principle in your life. In the hustle of daily demands, remember the tranquility of a Cypriot village square and the unhurried cadence of life.

Culinary Traditions: Infuse your meals with the flavors of Cyprus. Recreate the richness of Cypriot cuisine in your own kitchen, exploring recipes that have been passed down through generations. The act of cooking becomes a bridge that transports you back to the sunlit tavernas and bustling markets, connecting you to the island's culinary heritage.

Sustainable Living: Adopt sustainable practices inspired by the ecological consciousness of Cyprus. Reduce your environmental footprint, support local and ethical initiatives, and cultivate a sense of responsibility toward the planet. As you carry the lessons of sustainable living, you become a steward of the environments you traverse, ensuring they endure for future explorers.

The Unending Odyssey

The epilogue marks the end of this literary journey, but the odyssey of life continues. As you turn the final pages, consider that your exploration of Cyprus is not confined to the island's geographical boundaries. It's a narrative that intertwines with your personal story—a tapestry of experiences, connections, and self-discovery.

The Unwritten Chapters: As you bid farewell to Cyprus, acknowledge that the story doesn't conclude; it transforms. The chapters yet to be written are an invitation to explore new horizons, both external and internal. The uncharted territories of your future journeys hold the promise of discovery, just as each sunrise in Cyprus unveiled a new facet of its timeless beauty.

Kindred Spirits: Know that fellow travelers, whether they've traversed the same landscapes or explored different corners of the globe, are kindred spirits in this odyssey called life. Share your tales, listen to theirs, and recognize the interconnectedness that transcends borders.

In the shared language of exploration, you find a universal kinship that enriches the collective narrative of human experience.

A Tapestry of Endurance

As you close this chapter, envision the tapestry you've woven—the vibrant hues of cultural immersion, the intricate patterns of resilience, and the golden threads of shared joy. Your journey to Cyprus has not been a mere passage; it's been a creation, a collaboration with the island's landscapes, people, and stories.

Legacy of Connection: Consider the legacy you leave behind—a legacy of connection, goodwill, and shared moments. In the hearts of those you've encountered, in the places you've touched, your journey becomes an enduring imprint. Whether it's a smile exchanged in a village square or a shared laughter at a festival, these moments become timeless echoes in the tapestry of your legacy.

The Unfurling Tapestry: As you step away from the pages of this epilogue and into the uncharted expanse of your future, remember that the tapestry of your Cypriot adventure continues to unfurl. The echoes of ancient history, the aromas of Mediterranean cuisine, and the lessons of slow living become companions on your ongoing odyssey.

A Farewell, Yet Not Goodbye

In bidding farewell to Cyprus, recognize that it's not a final goodbye but a "kali antamosi"—a heartfelt until we meet again. The island's allure, with its timeless charm and enduring spirit, remains etched in your memories. As you carry Cyprus with you, may the echoes of your journey continue to resonate—a harmonious melody that accompanies you on the unending symphony of exploration.

The epilogue concludes, yet the narrative of your life's journey continues. Whether your path leads you back to Cyprus or toward new horizons, may each step be imbued with the wisdom gained, the connections forged, and the enduring spirit of exploration. As you embark on the unending odyssey, may your tapestry of experiences be a testament to a life well-lived—an odyssey that transcends time, borders, and the pages of this book.

And so, as the final chapter fades, may your journey be ever onward, ever unfolding—a tapestry of endurance, discovery, and fulfillment. Until we meet again on the road of life, safe travels, kindred explorer. May your story be a timeless ode to the beauty of the journey.

Appendix
Resources and Useful Information

Congratulations on reaching the end of "How to Move to Cyprus"! As you embark on your journey to the enchanting island, we understand the importance of having comprehensive resources at your fingertips. This appendix serves as a valuable toolkit, providing a compilation of resources and useful information to enhance your experience and ease your transition to Cyprus.

1. Government and Official Information:

- *Cyprus Government Portal:*
  - ○ Website: www.cyprus.gov.cy[1]
  - ○ A comprehensive resource for official government information, visa details, and essential services.
- *Ministry of Foreign Affairs:*
  - ○ Website: www.mfa.gov.cy[2]
  - ○ Access information on consular services, embassies, and diplomatic relations.

2. Visa and Residency:

- *Cyprus Migration Department:*
  - ○ Website: www.moi.gov.cy[3]
  - ○ Stay updated on visa requirements, residence permits, and immigration procedures.

3. Accommodation:

---

1. https://chat.openai.com/c/www.cyprus.gov.cy

2. https://chat.openai.com/c/www.mfa.gov.cy

3. https://chat.openai.com/c/www.moi.gov.cy

- *Cyprus Real Estate Portal:*
  - Website: www.cyprusrealestate.com.cy[4]
  - Explore housing options, rental properties, and real estate trends.
- *Airbnb:*
  - Website: www.airbnb.com[5]
  - Discover short-term accommodation options to kickstart your stay.

4. Job Market and Employment:

- *Cyprus Jobs:*
  - Website: www.cyprusjobs.com[6]
  - Browse job listings, post your resume, and connect with employers.
- *EURES Cyprus:*
  - Website: ec.europa.eu/eures
  - European Job Mobility Portal offering job opportunities and practical advice.

5. Education:

- *Ministry of Education, Culture, Youth, and Sports:*
  - Website: www.moec.gov.cy[7]
  - Obtain information on the education system, schools, and academic resources.
- *Universities and Higher Education:*
  - Explore local universities and educational

---

4. https://chat.openai.com/c/www.cyprusrealestate.com.cy

5. https://chat.openai.com/c/www.airbnb.com

6. https://chat.openai.com/c/www.cyprusjobs.com

7. https://chat.openai.com/c/www.moec.gov.cy

institutions for academic opportunities.

6. Healthcare:

- *Cyprus Ministry of Health:*
  - Website: www.moh.gov.cy[8]
  - Access healthcare services, insurance information, and medical facilities.

7. Financial Considerations:

- *Central Bank of Cyprus:*
  - Website: www.centralbank.cy[9]
  - Stay informed on financial regulations, currency exchange, and banking services.
- *Tax Department:*
  - Website: www.mof.gov.cy/tax
  - Understand tax obligations and access tax-related resources.

8. Language and Communication:

- *Language Learning Platforms:*
  - Explore language learning apps and online platforms to enhance your Greek language skills.

9. Cultural Integration:

- *Cyprus Cultural Services:*
  - Website: www.culture.gov.cy[10]
  - Learn about cultural events, heritage sites, and

---

8. https://chat.openai.com/c/www.moh.gov.cy

9. https://chat.openai.com/c/www.centralbank.cy

10. https://chat.openai.com/c/www.culture.gov.cy

community activities.

10. Transportation:

- *Cyprus Public Transport:*
    - ◦ Website: www.cyprusbybus.com[11]
    - ◦ Navigate public transportation options across the island.
- *Car Rentals:*
    - ◦ Explore car rental services for convenient travel within Cyprus.

11. Leisure and Recreation:

- *Cyprus Tourism Organization:*
    - ◦ Website: www.visitcyprus.com[12]
    - ◦ Discover tourist attractions, events, and recreational activities.

12. Safety and Emergency Contacts:

- *Emergency Services:*
    - ◦ Contact emergency services by dialing 112 for immediate assistance.
- *Embassy or Consulate Contacts:*
    - ◦ Keep the contact information for your country's embassy or consulate in Cyprus.

13. Expat Communities and Support:

- *Expat Forums and Social Groups:*
    - ◦ Join online expat forums and social groups to

11. https://chat.openai.com/c/www.cyprusbybus.com

12. https://chat.openai.com/c/www.visitcyprus.com

connect with the international community in Cyprus.

14. Legal and Practical Advice:

- *Legal Services:*
  - ○ Consult with local legal services for advice on residency, employment, and other legal matters.

15. Currency Exchange:

- *Currency Converter:*
  - ○ Utilize online currency converters to stay updated on exchange rates.

16. Further Reading:

- *Books and Literature:*
  - ○ Explore literature about Cyprus to deepen your understanding of its history, culture, and society.

17. Online Communities:

- *Social Media Groups:*
  - ○ Join expat and local social media groups for real-time information and community support.

18. Miscellaneous:

- *Weather Forecast:*
  - ○ Stay informed about the weather through reliable online weather forecast platforms.
- *Travel Insurance Providers:*
  - ○ Research and choose a reputable travel insurance provider for comprehensive coverage.

Remember, this appendix is a starting point, and the adventure ahead is yours to shape. Whether you're drawn to the historic sites, the vibrant culture, or the warmth of the people, Cyprus welcomes you with open arms. As you navigate this journey, may these resources serve as valuable companions, guiding you through the tapestry of experiences that await.

Safe travels, and may your time in Cyprus be a chapter filled with discovery, connection, and the fulfillment of your dreams!

Printed in Great Britain
by Amazon

41543663R00078